POLICE OFFICER STRESS AWARENESS AND MANAGEMENT

A Handbook for Practitioners

Robert J. Daniello

D1610004

Hamilton Books

A member of
The Rowman & Littlefield Publishing Group
Lanham · Boulder · New York · Toronto · Plymouth, UK

Copyright © 2011 by
Hamilton Books
4501 Forbes Boulevard
Suite 200
Lanham, Maryland 20706
Hamilton Books Acquisitions Department (301) 459-3366

Estover Road
Plymouth PL6 7PY
United Kingdom

Library of Congress Control Number: 2011923602
ISBN: 978-0-7618-5504-0 (paperback : alk. paper)
eISBN: 978-0-7618-5505-7

This handbook is dedicated to America's emergency service first responders in appreciation for their dedication, bravery, and consummate professionalism.

TABLE OF CONTENTS

List of Figures   vii

Foreword   ix

Preface   xi

Acknowledgements   xiii

Introduction   xv

Chapter One: The Psychosomatic Implications of Stress   1

Chapter Two: The General Sources of Stress in Policing   5

Chapter Three: Intragroup Stressors   11

Chapter Four: Organizational and Interpersonal Stressors   25

Chapter Five: Individual Stressors   33

Chapter Six: Perceived Stress and Length of Service   49

Chapter Seven: Selected Stress Management Strategies and   59
Coping Techniques

Glossary   85

References   89

Index   105

About the Author   110

LIST OF FIGURES

Figure 1.1: Components of the General Adaptation Syndrome   3

Figure 3.1: Major Roles of a Police Officer   19

Figure 5.1: Selected Solutions for Coping with Fear   39

Figure 5.2: Five Phases of a Crisis   43

Figure 6.1: Stages of a Police Officer's Career   50

Figure 6.2: The "Entry System"   55

Figure 7.1: Interorganizational Stressors   62

Figure 7.2: Situational Leadership in the Police Department   63

Figure 7.3: Stress Management Techniques   68

Figure 7.4: The Focus of EAPs   73

Figure 7.5: The CISD Team   78

Figure 7.6: The CISD Phases   79

FOREWORD

Rarely have I encountered more wisdom, so convincingly argued with a depth of feeling and knowledge of the subject, than outside the bindings of this manuscript. Dr. Daniello has made an outstanding contribution to the literature of stress in policing by clearly and concisely explaining why inappropriate responses to stress in the police forces of our nation pose a significant threat, not only to the officers themselves, but to their families, their departments, and to society in general. This particular area of police work has not received the attention it deserves from law enforcement practitioners across the country, despite the breadth and depth of the academic studies available on the topic.

This academic body of work has been immeasurably improved by Dr. Daniello's impressive study. It is hoped that his contribution will energize police departments across the nation to revisit selection criteria, recruit training, in-service training, and management training courses. Stress recognition, modern employee assistance programs, and stress reduction/coping techniques deserve to be at the top of the agenda for police executives concerned about the toll
improper stress coping techniques are taking on their departments.

With local government budgets under pressure for the foreseeable future, it is incumbent upon elected officials and appointed police executives to prudently manage all government resources. People are our greatest and most important resource. Nowhere is this more true than in police work. The human element is and always has been key to all successful police operational responsibilities, whether law enforcement, order maintenance, or public service. Dr. Daniello rightly points out that any executives who would use and discard employees as a means to an end are engaged in morally reprehensible conduct that may be successful in garnering short-term results, but will more likely than not result in long-term morale problems as well as psychological or physical difficulties for officers attempting to cope with stress this type of behavior causes.

Management-inflicted stress is cruel and unnecessary, coming as it does on the heels of the "normal" everyday stress faced by officers working shifts, responding to urgent calls for service, and handling critical incidents. Inappropriate officer responses to these stressors can result in higher absenteeism rates, a more cynical corps of officers, a less productive and a less efficient department, and early retirements for both health and other reasons. These are the known quantifiable costs. The hidden costs are visited upon society, the department, and the families of officers. Among those hidden costs are the losses of quality service to the community, less effective crime prevention, a possible increase in domestic violence cases involving officers, and a deterioration in the quality of family life for officers.

It is axiomatic that a police force composed of officers, managers, and supervisors, who have been trained to recognize stress in their own lives and how to appropriately cope with or manage their stress, and how not to unnecessarily increase stress in their subordinates will be more productive and cost the city, state, or county less in the long run. Morale will soar as satisfaction with work increases. Careers will be extended, officer health and family life can improve, and pension funds will become more fully funded with less early retirees due to stress-induced health-related retirements.

Dr. Daniello brings not only the rigor of his academic training and background to this timely study, but also the training and experience of his career as a law enforcement practitioner. His work is a "just right" blend of the theoretical and empirical. He, like many of us in law enforcement, has experienced and coped with the many stresses he describes and explains so effectively. He has observed fellow officers in distress and coping inappropriately with the rigors and strains that shift work, critical incidents, ineffective criminal justice system and the like place upon those of us who swear the oath to serve and protect. Unlike many of us, however, he has made it his mission to use the scientific method to mesh empirical observations with the theories that explain the why and how of stress and stress reduction strategies.

Dr. Daniello has conducted a longitudinal study of stress in police work and he refers to this study in this text. I would also suggest that extensive study should be conducted on the questions of functional (police-related) and situational (life changes) stressors that may increase or amplify the stresses that are reported in the longitudinal study. Which is to say that the level of stress that officers encounter may be amplified, regardless of their tenure in the department, by their assignment for example, or by the many life changes people experience during their working lives, or by any combination of these factors.

I found the discussion questions to be thought-provoking and had no trouble visualizing the use of this textbook in police academy training classes across the country. I also believe that the use of this manuscript merely as a class text would do it and Dr. Daniello a disservice. The wider audience is the vast sincere cadre of professional police executives and public officials with oversight authority for the operations of local police departments. These law enforcement officials will immediately recognize the truth of what Dr. Daniello has to say. Prudent law enforcement officials will take immediate steps to make stress identification, stress awareness and stress coping strategies department priorities as they lead our most important resources, our people, in the future.

Louis R. Anemone
Chief of Department, NYPD (retired)
April, 2010

PREFACE

The purpose of this handbook is to help police officers better understand and appropriately deal with the stressors they will experience throughout their careers. Although the stress of life can cause many serious consequences for all human beings, it is particularly harmful to police officers because being a police officer is understood to be one of the most stressful occupations. The stressors associated with their work are frequent, numerous, and cumulative. Each new stressor adds to an individual's stress level. While a single stressor may be relatively inconsequential in and of itself, if added to an already high level of stress, it can be debilitating (Robbins & Judge, 2007). The cumulative effects of stress are all too often harmful, not only to the individual police officer, but to the police department and to society as well. This handbook is intended to help police officers expand their knowledge about this real-world phenomenon.

Stress awareness, the causes (general and specific), and their consequences, are presented in the text. The reader will learn how perceived stress impacts a police officer's mental and physical well-being, and its concurrent influence on their morale and performance on the job. The reader will acquire an understanding of how stress affects a police officer's private life as well. Lastly, the reader will learn a number of appropriate coping mechanisms and stress management techniques that tend to mitigate the long-term risks that are linked to stress.

Robert J. Daniello
Cherry Hill, New Jersey
June, 2010

ACKNOWLEDGEMENTS

In the police profession, when rank and file members refer to a leader as a "cop's cop" it is an indication of the high esteem in which the recipient is held by members of the department. Chief Louis Anemeone will always be a cop's cop; admired and respected for his distinguished 34 year career, culminating with his elevation to Chief of Department, the NYPD's highest ranking uniformed police officer.

Chief Anemone earned a Bachelor Of Arts degree from the University of the State of New York, a Master's Of Arts degree from California State University, and is a graduate of the 20th session of the FBI National Executive Institute. He is a member of the International Association of Chiefs of Police, the International Association of Law Enforcement Intelligence Analysts, and is currently a law enforcement consultant and Chief Executive Officer of Anemone Consulting of Nanuet, New York. Among his numerous laudatory achievements, Chief Anemone is most famous for his role in implementing the world-renowned Compstat system in the NYPD.

I am most grateful to Chief Anemone for writing the Foreword to this handbook. For me it is a high honor, indeed. As in the past I will continue to seek his good counsel and guidance. I have the most profound respect for Chief Anemone and am proud to call him my friend.

My thanks to the University Press of America staff, particularly Ms. Brooke Bascietto, Associate Editor for her considerable support (and patience!) in helping bring a concept from proposal to publication. Kara Borbely formatted the text. Her considerable skills greatly exceed my own. I am fortunate to have had Kara as a partner in the project, and will be forever grateful for the guidance she generously provided.

Finally, I am grateful to the scholars who, over the past half-century, have presented their findings on the topic of stress and on the subject of workforce motivation. Their work is truly timeless. Any errors in the narrative are the result of my considerable imperfections and not those of any previous researcher cited in the text.

INTRODUCTION
SCOPE OF THE PROBLEM

Different things stress different people. If a sizeable number of people were asked what type of work induces the most stress, it is likely that many would say "being a cop." They would rationalize this opinion by pointing to the physical dangers associated with being a police officer. However, stress in the police profession is due primarily to psychological factors more so than to the physical aspects of the job. The realities of police work that include the work schedule, poor diet, sleep deprivation, and the lack of recreation and physical exercise, cause more harm to the police officer's health than injuries sustained in the line of duty (Reintzell, 1990).

The seriousness of a police officer's duties and responsibilities are both physically and mentally demanding (Eisenberg, 1975). Over the years researchers have theorized that police officers experience significant stress from their jobs and have established that law enforcement *is* one of the most stressful occupations in America (Eisenberg, 1975; Richard & Fell, 1975; Axelberd & Valle, 1978; Dash & Reiser, 1978; Goodin, 1978; Territo & Vetter, 1981). The real danger in policing may very well be related to the consequences of stress for the individual police officer. (Eisenberg, 1975; Webb & Smith, 1980; Terry, 1981; Shaeffer, 1985; Brown & Campbell, 1994; Martin, 1994).

One of the first consequences of stress is diminished job satisfaction; the greater the amount of stress, the lesser the job satisfaction (Martelli, Waters, & Martelli, 1989). Research conducted on the subject of police officer perceived stress consistently reveals that stress creates an adverse impact on the police officer, his or her family, and the ability of the department to carry out its mission (Farmer, 1990). Job-related stress can influence not only the health and performance of police officers, but also the morale and productivity of the entire organization (Scanlon, 1990; Violanti & Aron, 1993). Since stress can lead to the development of chronic conditions within a few years of its onset, (Williams, 2003), it makes good sense to lessen the unconstructive outcomes of stress, which will at the same time serve to improve the health and well-being of police officers (Harpold & Feemster, 2002).

How people feel about where they work, the work they do, and about themselves have significance on how they perform. In time, people under stress either resign or give up their expectation that work can be a fulfilling experience. They produce less and the quality of their work product is below standard. Morale and job satisfaction are conditions of employment that cannot be separated form productivity.

Fortunately, in the recent past there has been an increased awareness of, and an interest in, the causes and consequences of stress and the impact of stress on police officers (Kroes, 1985). More recently, critical incident stress (or post-traumatic stress) and early intervention strategies have been the subject of considerable research. The impact of major traumatic events can be readily understood. However, it is the ongoing, everyday, relatively minor stressful incidents that continuously bombard the police officer. The effects of these incremental stressors cause psychosomatic problems for the individual police officer and often result in their diminished performance. As a result, stress has emerged as a major topic in the study of police organizational behavior.

Job stress can be defined as an adaptive response to external stimuli resulting in physical and/or psychological consequences for organization members that can influence their behavior as well as their performance (Luthens, 1985). These dimensions are important to the understanding of job stress because dysfunctional stress (bad stress) can have damaging physiological and psychological consequences for employees. These undesirable outcomes are likely to adversely affect their health, attitude, and their contribution to the effectiveness of the organization (Steers, 1981).

Below are some of the major indicators of employee stress:

- Performance
    1. Lowered Productivity;
    2. Poor concentration;
    3. Signs of fatigue;
    4. Increased mistakes;
    5. Sporadic work pace; and
    6. Inconsistent work quality.
- Attendance
    1. Increased lateness;
    2. Increased absenteeism;
    3. Vague complaints of illness (leaving work early);
    4. Extended break/lunch periods; and
    5. Unexplained absences from the work station.
- Behavior
    1. Mood swings;
    2. Isolation;
    3. Apathy and indifference;
    4. Radical gain or loss of weight;
    5. Lowered morale;
    6. Deterioration of personal appearance; and
    7. Irritability.

- Safety
  1. High accident rate;
  2. Carelessness is evident;
  3. Needless risks taken; and
  4. Safety of colleagues neglected.

In 1992, Tang and Hammontree estimated that as much as 70 percent of absenteeism is due to stress-related illness. Stress can result not only in absenteeism, neglect, errors, and accidents but also in flawed decision-making. Stress can also lead to early retirement and is likely to lead to substance abuse and premature death (Luthens, 1985; Dixon, 1988; Brown & Campbell, 1990; Kureczka, 1996). Although unsubstantiated by quantitative data, there may be a link between the frustrations experienced at work and the rising drug use in the United States (Karasek & Theorell, 1990). Stress can also lead to domestic disputes, possible violence between partners, and divorce (Blackmore, 1978; Danto, 1978; Singleton & Teahan, 1978; Kennedy-Ewing, 1989). Police officers are certainly not excluded from any of the aforementioned possibilities.

Perceived stress in policing and its underlying causes make the police officer's job typically more stressful than most other occupations. The emotional impact of police work is complex and sometimes overwhelming. All too often it is more powerful than the police officer's psychological defenses to cope with it. While the causes and consequence of stress are manifold, there is a sufficient understanding to believe that much of the stress experienced by police officers can be properly managed.

ORGANIZATION OF THE NARRATIVE

Chapter One provides the reader with the foundation of a theoretical and empirical understanding of stress along with an account of the psychosomatic consequences associated with perceived stress. Chapter Two presents the underlying causes of perceived stress in policing. Chapter Three acquaints the reader with selected stressors that are caused by police work itself and by the working conditions within the police organization. Chapter Four suggests the reasons why the organization itself is a major cause of police officer perceived stress, and concludes with an explanation of how a police officer interprets certain stress-provoking aspects of the job. Chapter Five identifies several individual stressors and their characteristics that generate anxiety and tension.

Chapter Six discusses the relationship between perceived stress and length of service. Chapter Seven concludes the text by disclosing several coping mechanisms that are available to police officers who suffer from the harmful effects of perceived stress. Each chapter ends with a set of discussion questions.

References are cited within the text as well as alphabetically listed in the Bibliography and Reference section at the end of the narrative according to the guidelines and standards incorporated in the Publication Manual of the American Psychological Association (Washington, D.C., 6th Ed., 2010). The APA manual is used primarily as a guide for the dissemination of knowledge in the social and behavioral sciences. Since scientific knowledge represents the accomplishments of scores of researchers over time, the intent of a Literature Review is to acquaint the reader with numerous sources of information on a particular topic (p.169). As such, the narrative includes an exhaustive list of citations. The citations and the succeeding reference list provide the reader with the opportunity to retrieve the sources of information for their own researches.

CHAPTER ONE
THE PSYCHOSOMATIC
IMPLICATIONS OF STRESS

OVERVIEW

The opening chapter of the text provides the reader with the foundation of a theoretical and empirical understanding of stress in our lives. The narrative also describes how the body and the mind act in response to stressors and includes a description of the associated health risks. The chapter makes clear one very important lesson: The risks identified with the phenomenon of perceived stress can range from a relatively short-term nuisance (perhaps a headache) to the very real possibility of death. Since police officers experience a multitude of work related stressors, they are particularly susceptible to the risks that correlate with stress.

THE PHYSICAL AND PSYCHOLOGICAL
CONSEQUENCES OF STRESS

The term *stress* refers to a person's reaction to a disturbing factor, or set of factors, in the environment. It is defined as an adaptive response to an external situation that results in physiological, psychological, and behavioral deviations. It relates to an imbalance between the demands made on an individual and his or her capabilities to meet those demands. Stress can be overwhelming if there is no suitable outlet provided for releasing the excess tension produced within the human mind and body. It is clear that when perceived stress levels are beyond a person's ability to cope, the emotional tension manifests itself in psychosomatic consequences.

Luthens, Folkman, and DeLonis (1988) reported that "Stress itself is not a simple variable, but a system of interdependent processes, including appraisal and coping, which mediate the frequency, intensity, duration, and type of psychological and somatic response" (p. 486). Stress is essentially a biological response to a stimulus and is not necessarily harmful. There is "good" stress and "bad" stress (Luthens, 1985). As early as 1908, Yerkes and Dodson reported that very low or very high stress levels were debilitating, while moderate stress levels enhance alertness, motivation, and performance. In fact, relatively short-term exposure can actually be beneficial. "Good" stress is stress that can be managed. For example, the stress of competing in an athletic contest often stimulates performance. When there is no attempt to cope with stress, particularly with "bad" stress, or a feeling of an inability to cope persists, harm is done to the individual (Howard & Joint, 1994).

Selye (1956) found that stress causes certain changes in the structure and chemical composition of the human body. "Bodily changes during stress act upon mentality and vice versa (p. 367). According to Selye, the psychosomatic implications of stress are numerous and include, but are not necessarily limited to, the following:

- Headaches;
- Digestive diseases;
- Ulcers;
- Hypertension;
- High blood pressure;
- Cardiovascular disease;
- Metabolic diseases;
- Sexual derangements;
- Nervous disorders;
- Inflammation diseases of the skin and eyes;
- Allergic and hypersensitivity diseases;
- Rheumatoid arthritis;
- Cancer; and
- Production of an excess of both adrenalines and corticoids.

The production of adrenalines and corticoids can cause a person to be virtually intoxicated by his or her own stress hormones. This sort of drunkenness may cause more harm to the individual and to society than the alcoholic kind. If the adrenal must produce an excess of corticoids to maintain life during periods of stress, it is likely that the resulting excess hormone itself may have dangerous consequences.

Following the research of Selye, Ellison and Genz (1983) found that the perception of stress is more consequential than the actual events themselves. Gaillard and Wientjes (1994) concluded that stress may affect the course of many, if not all, diseases. Chronic stress was found to constitute a danger to the well-being and health of individuals as long-term stress reduces the body's ability to fend off illness. "Flooding" the body with any hormone produces disease. According to O'Neill, Hanewicz, Fransway, and Cassidy-Riske (1982) "very task the body performs exacts a little wear and tear. As these demands accelerate in frequency or intensity, the wear and tear responds correspondingly" (p. 389). Increased heart rate, systolic blood pressure, and actual tissue damage are among the health risks (Alkus & Padesky, 1983). Stress may also cause changes in regulatory mechanisms and lead to tissue damage as well as provoking the development of malignant processes, or suppression of the immune system. This condition has been associated with different levels of dysfunction and disease, ranging from minor and temporary nuisances to manifest illnesses that sometimes may be fatal.

Moreover, Howard and Joint (1994) found that stress can also result in mental disorders. After an accumulation of stressors, the body essentially breaks down resulting in functional failures (O'Neill, et al., 1982).

According to Mitchell (1986b), "the ability to remember, think clearly, make decisions, and perform calculations and other highly cognitive functions is impaired by stress" (p. 24).

Hans Selye, a leading authority on stress and author of the 1956 classic work entitled, *The Stress of Life*, maintained that life is a process of adaptation to the circumstances present in the environment and that the general response to stressful events follow a fairly consistent pattern known as the General Adaptation Syndrome (GAS). The GAS consists of three phases, which he characterized as an evolutionary process during the life of every person from birth to death. Selye and later Anderson, Swenson, and Clay (1995) identified three phases of stress in humans symbolized in the following figure:

Figure 1.1: Components of the General Adaptation Syndrome.

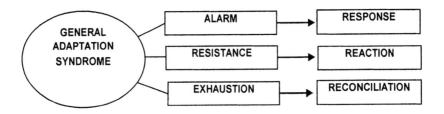

The first phase is the alarm response phase in which the body mobilizes energy to react to a situation. The alarm response phase includes an increased pulse rate, an increased tendency to sweat, the tensing of the forehead and neck muscles, eye strain, fluttering eyelids, irregular and shallow breathing, cold hands, and "butterflies" in the stomach. When exposure to a stress-producing situation continues for a protracted period, the alarm phase is followed by the resistance response phase.

In the resistance response phase the body is prepared for the fight-or-flight response. Here the body seems to develop a resistance to the particular stress that is provoking the alarm phase. In short, the body reacts and adjusts to the situation. The third stage is exhaustion phase.

The exhaustion phase occurs from repeated stressors over time. If not mitigated appropriately, psychosomatic symptoms may result. Sometimes during a stressful event a point is reached where the body can no longer maintain its resistance. Many of the emotional responses that originally appeared in the alarm phase begin to reappear. Normally, the body is able to cope with the stressful situation. At this interval the various physiological activities that are accelerated in the emotion of the situation return to normal levels. Sometimes, however, the emotion-provoking situation continues indefinitely and cannot be easily discharged. If the stress persists, or the person fails to adequately cope with the stress, maladies such as chronic depression, feelings of fatigue, or alienation may evidence itself. Consequently, severe physiological and psychological problems are likely to occur once the individual's defenses have collapsed at the exhaustion phase. Exhaustion overcomes an individual's coping mechanisms (Standfest, 1996).

DISCUSSION QUESTIONS

1.   What is meant by the term "psychosomatic," and how does it differ from the specific physiological and psychological symptoms associated with stress?

2.   Why is the perception of stress more harmful than the actual event itself?

3.   How can the so-called "good" stress significantly benefit a police officer?

4.   Give an example of a fight-or-flight situation a police officer is likely to encounter on the job. What should be the police officer's appropriate reaction?

5.   Researchers have identified three phases of stress in humans, referred to as the General Adaptation Syndrome. Identify each phase by incorporating an example of a real-world stressful incident in your explanation. What can be done for the individual if the emotion-provoking situation cannot be easily discharged?

CHAPTER TWO
THE GENERAL SOURCES OF STRESS
IN POLICING

OVERVIEW

In the present chapter the reader will learn about the perceived stressors associated with policing and their underlying causes that make the police officer's job more stressful than most occupations.

INHERENT STRESSORS

Not unlike the general population, police officers are stressed by everyday events in their lives (Stotland, 1991). People experience various forms of stress at home, at work, and in social settings. Police officers experience stresses the same as others, but also in ways much different from the average citizen.

People choose a career in policing in part because of the prospects of adventure and excitement; they like to help people in distress, and are further attracted to policing for its job security, and its general compensation package, such as salary, benefits, and the retirement provisions of the profession (Storch & Panzarella, 1996). However, people entering police work quickly learn that it is a high stress occupation (Band & Manuele, 1987; Dantzer, 1987), and that police officers are subjected to an inordinate amount of work-related stress throughout their careers (Teten & Minderman, 1977; Adams, McTernan, & Remsberg, 1980; Kurke, 1995). In choosing police work as an occupation, people thus consciously or unconsciously select a vocation with inherent and powerful job stressors (Boyd, 1994); they experience stress as they perform their traditional duties shouldering responsibility for others in emergency situations along with the fear, anxiety, and conflicting pressures that occur during each working day of their careers (Yukl, 1981).

Police officers belong to a profession that is commonly viewed as an occupation high in psychic-battering. That is, a continual condition of conflict-induced occurrences: at one end of the spectrum there is violence and fear while at the other end, monotony and inactivity. While the potential for excitement is omnipresent, police officers, particularly those "working the street," also go through protracted periods of boredom (down time) during a typical tour of duty. Both are difficult to reconcile (Machell, 1993). Nevertheless, it is the *opportunity* for excitement that tends to attract applicants to the job. Although a primary requisite of all individuals who aspire to be police officers is the emotional stability to withstand all of the stressors of the job (Ostrov, 1986), most candidates enter police service without the knowledge of the various and sundry stressors that, over time, often result in physical and mental health consequences for practitioners (Boyd, 1994).

When stress surfaces, it manifests itself in a variety of ways that are both physiological and psychological (Evans, Coman, & Stanley, 1992). The greatest risks of policing are the psychological stressors associated with the job, rather than assaultive criminals (Wilson, McLaren, Fyfe, Greene, & Walsh, 1997). Previous research by Alkus and Padesky (1983) confirmed that, although the physical hazards of the job are not to be ignored, the most significant risks to police officers are psychological in nature.

Police work reflects a particular psychological outlook that has important consequences for the health and well-being of those who perform it. Whether police officers are subjected to more sources of stress compared with other occupations has not as yet been firmly established (Alkus & Padesky, 1983; Ostrov, 1986; Hart, Wearing, & Headey, 1995). The police profession in many ways, however, is unlike any other occupation. Innumerable assignments are tension-filled, distasteful, dangerous, and intrinsically stress-provoking. The danger, violence, and tragedy experienced by police officers result in added levels of stress not typically experienced by the general population. Society relies upon the police to intervene in and resolve a plethora of problems ranging from public nuisance complaints to tactical contingencies; from routine investigations of crimes that have occurred previously to high-risk, felony-in-progress crimes (the latter considered to be a significant cause of stress for police officers [Westmorland & Haddock, 1989]); from petty disorderly misconduct to domestic violence; from minor traffic accidents to mass-casualty incidents; from barking dogs to vicious animal attacks. Police officers must also function as social workers, guidance counselors, sidewalk psychologists, and thoughtful negotiators (Kline, 1989). One minute the police officer is viewed as the proverbial "knight in shining armor," the next minute a fire-breathing dragon. This complex, albeit unofficial job description, and the role ambiguity associated with being a police officer heighten stress levels and concomitant pressures that are unequal to any other occupation (Kroes, Margolis, & Hurrell, 1974a; Fell, Richard, & Wallace, 1980; Terry, 1981; Reese, 1986). According to Wexler and Logan (1983), police officers see a side of life that most of the population rarely, if ever, encounters.

Compounding an already burdensome set of responsibilities, police officers are considered to be on duty 24-hours a day, even when technically off duty. They are expected to intervene appropriately whenever they witness an act of misconduct (Bahn, 1984; Blau, 1994). Working in extreme weather conditions

and the threat of exposure to environmental hazards are frequently cited as causes of stress (Kennedy-Ewing, 1989). Along with the dangers and threats
commonly associated with policing, problems concerning the enforcement of
laws, police department policies and procedures, agency rules and regulations,
tours of duty (particularly rotating shifts), and the quasi-military structure of the
department produce a unique set of stressors separate from the rigors of the
work itself (Symonds, 1969).

Over the years police officers continue to complain that the principal cause
of police officer stress is related to administrative matters—the police department itself (Storch & Panzarella, 1996). The police department bureaucracy and
its organizational practices have been found to be significant stressors that
compound an already potentially overwhelming set of working conditions
(Kroes, Margolis, & Hurrell, 1974b; Hillgren, Bond, & Jones, 1976; Robinette,
1987; Thrash, 1990; Crank & Caldero, 1991; Hart, Wearing, & Headey, 1993;
Hart, et al, 1995; Violanti & Aron, 1995; Storch & Panzarella, 1996; Wilson, et
al, 1997). Most police officers can handle the bombardment of incoming
stressors most of the time. Many assert that it is the bosses that make their work
(and lives) more difficult.

Police officers assigned to patrol operations are particularly susceptible to
complications associated with stress. Their work is usually more dangerous and
may be more stressful than that of their colleagues in other assignments (Brooks,
Piquero, & Cronin, 1994). Handling street-level calls for service during an
unusually active and demanding tour of duty often adds to the pressures of the
job. Contrast this condition with an uneventful, quiet tour of duty. Police officers assigned to basic patrol operations spend a substantial portion of their tour of
duty driving radio patrol cars. Even the routine operation of a motor vehicle over
a long period of time has the potential to cause stress due to a combination of
factors that include concentration, anxiety, physical discomfort, and monotony
that can result in a sleep-like loss of awareness (Selye, 1956; Howard & Joint,
1994).

Physical exhaustion can also be extended to mental fatigue, a cognitive
weariness resulting from prolonged cerebral concentration or boredom. Fatigue
is one of the major modifiers of job stress in police work. The possible consequences of fatigue are made more severe by the complex nature of the police
officer's occupational environment. Fatigue tends to lower the quality of the
decision making process and thus increases the probability that a less than
optimal decision will be made. Fatigue adversely affects both the emergent and
routine aspects of the job on a continuum.

The more complex or stressful the situation, the greater the detrimental
effects of fatigue (Graham-Bonnalie, 1972). Fatigue decreases a police officer's
capacity to discern, analyze, and act appropriately upon complex situational
variables that are present in every emergency. It also contributes to accident

proneness particularly during periods of low activity, and increases the likelihood of a stress-related illness.

Police officers are highly visible in society and are exposed to dangers making them continually aware of facing the unknown. Because any situation can result in injury or death to themselves or others, police officers must be in a constant state of alertness. The need for quick, accurate judgment and heightened awareness are common conditions of the job. This state of constant readiness, by itself, has been found to be an unremitting source of stress for the police officer (Selye, 1956; Symonds, 1969). The so-called "good stress," for example, prepares police officers responding to reports of crimes-in-progress by heightening their awareness of surroundings, increasing their sense of sight, smell, and sound, and, by drawing on their training and experience in approaching the scene. Police officers clearly benefit from good stress, which is generally considered to be temporary in duration. Conversely, "bad" stress is stress that lasts long enough, or is of sufficient intensity that one's body can no longer manage it. Situationally induced stress can improve task performance to a point. But even good stress can have a deleterious affect once individual thresholds are crossed. Police officers cannot afford to let this stress get out of control. Their lives and the lives of others depend on their ability to respond effectively under duress.

The jobs that are most likely to produce stress and its resultant physiological manifestations, particularly heart disease, are those that combine great demands with little control (Karasek & Theorell, 1990). It should be that police work includes both of these characteristics, perhaps more than in any other public sector occupation. For example, in a study of stress and strain among police officers, firefighters, and a diverse group of non-emergency government employees, Pendleton, Stotland, Spiers, and Kirsch (1989) found that police officers reported significantly more stress than the other groups.

The effects of stress can be likened to the slow eroding processes found in nature. Gradually, stress wears down the physical health and the emotional well-being of many police officers. These consequences surely affect the general population. For the police, however, the nature of the job and the continuous exposure to stressful situations can result in ominous consequences for the individual police officer, for his or her family, and for society. According to Alkus and Padesky (1983),

> Police officers experience a greater incidence of health problems than most other occupations. Circulatory and digestive disorders, especially coronary heart disease, are significantly higher among police officers than comparison groups. Psycho-physiological disturbances commonly found with police include skin disorders, muscle cramps, tension headaches, bronchial asthma, hyperventilation, ulcers, genitourinary and endocrine disorders. Lower back pain and late onset of diabetes also are significantly higher than in other (p. 58).

To reiterate, police officers, in the performance of their duties, face a wide-range of stressful situations and events that occur over a prolonged period of time that are outside the realm of normal experience and have the capacity to cause significant personal distress (McCafferty, Domingo, & McCafferty, 1989; Evans, Coman, & Stanley, 1992). The precise degree to which "the job" produces stress is not entirely known and probably varies among individual police officers. It is, nonetheless, generally agreed that the job is very stressful and likely the cause of many health problems encountered by police officers.

Stress is a part of everyday life; it is pervasive in all occupations. However, unlike other occupations in which stressors might be eliminated, avoided, or reduced, police officers only have one option: learning more effective coping strategies (Violanti & Marshall, 1983; Tang & Hammontree, 1992). Unfortunately, previous studies have shown that police officers tend to use inappropriate coping mechanisms to deal with perceived stress. These include withdrawal, emotional blocking, alcohol and drug abuse, recalcitrant behavior, and cynicism (Ball, 1986). Alcohol and drug abuse have been linked to workplace stress and it is a major problem for police officers seeking relief from stress. In fact, many stress-related problems are likely to become alcohol or drug problems. Alcohol in particular is an escape into the euphoria of fantasy, rather than facing the problem of reality. It is a way of "numbing out." Another significant reason for the high level of alcohol consumption among police officers is the pressure from the peer group to drink as a way of reconciling the distress of the job and proving one's masculinity. What is more, too much stress can cause sleep deprivation as well (Selye, 1956).

Alkus and Padesky (1983) determined that it is not necessarily the source or type of stress that leads to physical and psychological disability, but the manner in which such stress is handled or released. The goal of stress management, therefore, is not to eliminate stress, but to control it. Its aim is to moderate needless and debilitating stress that police officers encounter when they are striving to perform their duties.

DISCUSSION QUESTIONS

1. Give an example of a repetitive stressor typically experienced by police officers. Explain your answer.

2. With reference to the above example, in your opinion, what can be done to limit or reduce the particular stressor?

3. Police work has always been considered one of the most exciting and rewarding occupations. If this is true, why is the job so stressful? If the job is so stressful, why are so many men and women attracted to it? What can be done to

make the job less stressful or at least reduce the influence of stressors on police officers throughout their careers? What are some of the consequences if we fail to do this?

CHAPTER THREE
INTRAGROUP STRESSORS

OVERVIEW

Chapter Three is the first segment of a three-part discussion of selected stressors that are caused primarily by the nature of the work itself and by the nature of the police organization. In 1988, Dr. John Violanti presented a model of stressors peculiar to the police environment. The model categorized police stressors into four groupings: Intragroup Stressors, Organizational Stressors, Interpersonal Stressors, and Individual Stressors. The Violanti model will form the framework for the discussion.

Intragroup Stressors include the following:

- The discrepancy between the police conception of justice and the actual working of the criminal justice system;
- Conflicts between the police officer's role as social controller and community helper; and
- Strains on family relations.

We begin the discussion of intragroup stressors with the causes and consequences of police officer behavior and its impact on family and friends.

RELATIONSHIPS WITH FAMILY AND FRIENDS

Attitudes toward the workplace are influenced by both work and non-work domains. Williams (2003) learned that the combination of work responsibilities and family obligations can lead to stress. Stress is also a prime suspect in the increase of marital discord that further complicates work stress (Mitchell, 1986b). Work-related role stress and work-family conflicts can influence the attitudes of employees toward their jobs (Boles, Johnston, & Hair, 1997). Howard, Donofrio, and Boles (2004) found that the conflict between work and family obligations is closely related to job satisfaction. These correlations can be discovered in any occupation. However, working conditions in the police occupation have a propensity to operate against a successful marriage (Alkus &

Padesky, 1983). While job stressors impact police officers directly, it is acknowledged that police officers will bring that stress home to the family. Anything that stresses the police officer has the potential to stress the family, and vice versa (Gudjonsson & Adlam, 1985; Brown & Campbell, 1990; Bryant 1990; Albrecht, 1992). According to White and Honig (1995), a complex, cyclical relationship exists between the work life and home life of a police officer with each impacting and being impacted by the other.

Blau (1994) and White and Honig (1995) reported that when a police officer walks through the door, he or she brings home the stress accumulated on the job. The constant exposure to fear and danger can increase anxiety and manifest itself in a number of ways within the family, including increased irritability and a lowered tolerance for aggravation. Police officers tend to take home the anger and frustration related to work stressors, displacing them into their relationships. Spouses watch the anger and frustration from work unexpectedly vented in the home in the form of criticism of family members (Alkus & Padesky, 1983). Jackson and Maslach (2007) found that police officers who experience elevated stress levels on the job were more likely to exhibit behaviors within the family that include the following:

- Being angry;
- Wanting to avoid involvement in family affairs;
- Wanting to spend more time away from the family; and
- Having unhappy marriages.

Although family members are not directly exposed to the ordeals of police work, police officers may want to discuss work incidents with the spouse and family members as a way of reducing stress. At the end of the workday, the accumulated level of tension can be reduced by simply discussing the events of the day. This stress-reduction technique forms the basis of treatment in virtually every school of psychotherapy. However, the police officer is confronted with the confidential nature of the work and the very real possibility that any discussion might be turned into gossip by family members. In reality, while a discussion about the day's events may be somewhat therapeutic for the police officer, it has the potential to transfer the police officer's stress to family members.

On the other hand, many police officers are generally reluctant to discuss job-related matters with the family because they may believe the details of anxiety-provoking workday experiences, if expressed at home, will create problems for their spouses. There is often a desire to protect loved ones from the harsh realities of the job (Teten & Minderman, 1977). Therefore, the police officer must leave the job behind at headquarters and change to the role of husband, wife, father, or mother before walking through the door of their home (Bonifacio, 1991). Other family problems can arise when police officers have trouble switching from their job-related roles to their roles as family members.

For example, police officers are socialized in many ways on the job to demonstrate loyalty to the department by relying exclusively on one another rather than the family for support (Hageman, 1978). This approach results in yet another incongruity in the police officer-family relationship.

The notorious solidarity that exists among police officers arises to a large degree from a feeling of isolation. As a result of this condition, police officers typically socialize with other police officers.

When groups of police officers get together, they tend to "talk shop." Police officers are often unable or unwilling to express their true feelings to family and friends. They tend to believe that only fellow police officers can understand and appreciate their relevant and unique set of issues and problems. Consequently, police officers tend to share important feelings only with other police officers, and receive feedback and direction from only one source, a source whose views are usually the same. Thus, the police officer is rarely exposed to different ideas or perspectives. In turn, the police officer's family comes to view him or her as a one-dimensional person.

Many situations experienced by police officers cause them to lose faith in others. They are likely to develop an "us-versus-them" view of society. Soon they may begin to trust only other police officers; the only people they believe fully understand how the world really is. Some may gradually withdraw from their family, relatives, and friends, and socialize with fewer and fewer people outside of the job (Graves, 1996). The professional and social demands of police work may regulate the police officer's family and friends to a secondary status that often results in alienation (Reintzell, 1990). As police officers become more secretive, emotionally distant, and less involved with the family, a gradual isolation from family and friends often results (Parker & Roth, 1973; Reiser, 1974a; Stratton, 1975; Stratton, 1978; Hageman, 1978; Maynard & Maynard, 1980; Alkus & Padesky, 1983). According to Alkus and Padesky (1983), the police officer's social involvement with non-police friends is likely to be reduced for many reasons:

> Due to the danger inherent in his [her] work, the officer learns to be constantly attentive to those signs indicating a potential for violence or crime. As a result, he or she becomes a "suspicious" person and less desirable as a friend. In some cases, the norms of friendship may directly conflict with duty. Police suffer personal rejection as a function of their job and may be oversensitive to signs of hostility. Some friends and neighbors will approach them during leisure hours to solve problems or handle emergencies. Other neighbors may deride them.
>
> Finally, there is the ever-present problem of scheduling social events when not working "normal" hours (p. 58).

As indicated above, one of the most frequently reported occupational risks of the job is that the police officer's friends tend to treat him or her differently. Acquaintances begin reassessing relationships. Police officers at the same time become emotionally detached from social contacts in part as a defense mechanism to help them cope with some of the more personally horrifying aspects of the job (Evans, et al., 1992).

The police officer's behavior at home can also become one of indifference, contempt, and hostility (Bonifacio, 1991). All of the stated influences create stress, and work in opposition to the goals of building intimate relationships (Borum & Philpost, 1993). As a result of these conditions, as previously indicated, police officers spend an increasing amount of off-duty time with their fellow police officers, turning to their peers and becoming enmeshed in the police subculture. With peers, police officers feel that they can talk freely and be understood. More often than not, the police officer refuses to discuss work problems with his or her spouse (Alkus & Padesky, 1983). Former New York City Police Commissioner William Bratton characterized this condition as being wrapped up in the blue cocoon (Bratton, 1998). This clannishness promotes the perception that the police officer's colleagues are the most important people fostering the idea of "sticking together," even to the exclusion of the spouse (Stratton, 1975).

There is a downside to an over reliance on the peer group for shelter. In the police organization, social needs and pressures can create stress. For example, the police officer's peer group may impose pressure to conform and adopt the attitudes and value systems of the organization, particularly early in his or her career. Individual police officers who do not conform to group norms may be excluded from social and work groups, and even ridiculed by their peers. These troubling aspects can lead to poor interrelationships at work that are certain to be stressful for police officers (Williams, 2003). They may experience social isolation from the one group they desperately need. The pressure to conform may be intense. In 2003, Collins and Gibbs found that the organizational subculture is a key issue in police officer stress.

According to Kurke (1995), the organization's value system and the needs and value system of the individual must be in harmony to avoid further stress. Regardless of the psychological reinforcers present in the police subculture, social support across both work and home environments is very important (Freedy & Hobfoll, 1994). In spite of the roadblocks to relationships, the police officer must maintain ties with the so-called civilian world. Since deficient social support directly causes stressful conditions that increase the incidence of physiological and psychological strain, the lack of social support would be itself considered a stressor (Luthans, 1985; Kaufmann & Beehr, 1989). In the final analysis, the key to being a successful police officer is balancing the desire to be a police officer with the needs and responsibilities of a personal life.

Police departments are paramilitary organizations. One potential risk of being associated with the paramilitary structure of the police organization is the onset of rigidity and authoritarianism that begins almost immediately during entry-level orientation and training. A number of studies indicate that police officers rank high on authoritarianism (Evans, et al, 1992). A natural extension of this condition is for the police officer to give orders at home and expect immediate and unconditional compliance, which can become offensive to family members (White & Honig, 1995). The traits and dispositions such as image, control, discipline, emotional detachment, and suspicion that make exceptional police officers are often transferred to personal situations in such a way that they can be destructive. The disposition to take charge when acted out in a family relationship may cause the police officer to be a dominating spouse and an authoritarian parent. For example, police officers are sometimes frustrated by an untidy, less-than-perfect home (Shearer, 1993), and may have explicit, unambiguous, and unwavering behavioral requirements for his or her children who are expected to conform to clearly established in-home rules and regulations. Although police officers assume they are necessary and appropriate, professional dispositions on the job are often inappropriate at home. The professional disposition builds respect and confidence on the job; in the family relationship, however, it builds a wall resulting in the police officer feeling alienated and alone. The belief in the need to maintain a professional image tends to keep family and friends at a distance (Southworth, 1990).

By necessity, police officers work within a framework of violence and suspicion. They experience growing suspiciousness and pessimism as they move through their careers (Alkus & Padesky, 1983). As a result, police officers tend to be cynical and suspicious of individuals they meet while performing their duties. There is an underlying attitude of distrust. This mindset can cross over the boundary into family life as well (Stratton, 1975). By questioning everything, spouses and children become suspects in every family encounter (Southworth, 1990). Police officers may virtually cross-examine a child about recent activities, or become preoccupied with the idea a spouse is unfaithful.

Police officers tend to be overprotective of their family as well (Stratton, 1975), and become restrictive when it comes to the activities of a child or a spouse. This is a result of their constant exposure to deception, victimization, and violence; they become more fearful on behalf of their families (White & Honig, 1995). This trepidation for the safety and well-being of their family is a direct result of what they observe at work (Alkus & Padesky, 1983). To summarize, many police officer-family relationships are destroyed by bringing home the interrogating, ordering, and suspicious behavior that is developed from hard experiences on the street. Concomitantly, the family is regularly distressed by the police officer's need to be in command.

Police officers are often absent from the home during significant times in the lives of their children (Alkus & Padesky, 1983; Blau, 1994). Lack of availability as a parent can result in resentment on the part of the children. Coupled with the decreased trust, overprotectiveness, and an autocratic demeanor, the overwhelmed police officer may resent the demands of his or her children, becoming irritable when interaction finally occurs resulting in tension and conflict between police officers and their children. Such a restrictive approach can lead to rebellion on the part of adolescents. Compounding these internal family problems, children are often ostracized outside of the home, especially during adolescence because a parent is a police officer (Alkus & Padesky, 1983; White & Honig, 1995).

Reports of scandals and investigations of misconduct, whether founded or unfounded, time and again impact on morale and decrease their self-esteem further alienating police officers from the public. This condition does not limit the distress to the police officer. Spouses share the humiliation of the scandal or the investigation of an alleged act of wrongdoing. They often represent the couple at social events and feel the pressure to defend their police officer spouse from criticism (White & Honig, 1995).

Police families must also deal with the ever-present possibility that serious injury or death could result from the job (Alkus & Padesky, 1983; Mantell, 1986; Wittrup, 1986). Each time a husband or wife sends a police officer spouse to work, the issue of danger surges to the foreground. For some family members, the police officer's firearm can be a constant reminder of the dangers intrinsic in the job (Alkus & Padesky, 1983; White & Honig, 1995). For a spouse, having a firearm in the house raises concerns about safety for themselves and their children as well.

Police officers and their families live with the knowledge that criminal offenders are often armed with superior firepower, which creates an occupational stressor that impacts their personal lives (Witkin, Geist, & Friedman, 1990). Compounding the threat of injury or death from a weapon, police officers fear the risk of contracting diseases such as AIDS, Hepatitis, and tuberculosis and transmitting these diseases to family members (Hammett, 1987). The police officer's feelings of invincibility are shattered when he or she sustains an injury or suffers an infirmity on the job. With the exception of experiencing a line-of-duty death of a coworker, being injured or infirmed are among the most distressing experiences in police work (Bonifacio, 1991).

The financial status of the police officer's family relies on the salary and the opportunities for advancement. The family's quality of life is tied to the police officer's status on the job. Police officers may need to work overtime or acquire a second job to supplement their income in order to support the family (Alkus & Padesky, 1983). The financial stability of the family may be threatened if the police officer makes an error in judgment that results in disciplinary action and/or civil litigation. When they make mistakes, they face increasing internal scrutiny, more so than ever before (Larsson & Starrin, 1988). The consequences of error can be extreme, including the loss of job and income, which can be devastating to the security of the family (White & Honig, 1995).

Having a spouse secure a special duty assignment can be source of pride for the family as well as a source of additional income. However, the elevated status and the pay increase may be seen as inadequate compensation for the debt incurred in terms of the inconvenience and the decreased amount of time the police officer may have for his or her family (White & Honig, 1995). For example, the work orientations and habits developed by undercover officers often have spillover effects on their interpersonal relations with family and friends (Pogrebin & Poole, 1993). Many spouses also report being concerned that their police officer husband/wife is spending long hours with a person of the opposite sex. This condition can be uncomfortable or even threatening. Police partners share a special bond that can generate envy or jealousy in a spouse (White & Honig, 1995). Of course, this form of association is not limited to special duty assignments.

Irregular and unpredictable hours prevent or disrupt the stability needed for family planning (Alkus & Padesky, 1983). This condition of employment occurs regardless of the police officer's duty assignment in the department. White and Honig (1995) reported that the work schedule is one of the top complaints of spouses of police officers. Work schedules, long hours, end-of-tour arrests, on-call time, court appearances, and mandatory overtime often result in last minute changes of plans that are disruptive for the family (Alkus & Padesky, 1983; O'Neill & Cushing, 1991; Borum & Philpot, 1993; Kannady, 1993). A police officer who objects to working a particular shift or assignment because of family discord is often perceived as being disloyal to the department and having skewed priorities (White & Honig, 1995).

Further, during large-scale emergencies, police officers are expected to attend to the needs of the community without first being allowed to verify the well-being of their own family members. This circumstance has been mitigated by the availability of cellular telephone communications, provided the system is functioning as designed during the emergency. Nevertheless, the policy forces police officers to choose between their obligations as public servants and their roles and responsibilities as parents and spouses. When emergent situations occur, families receive a clear message that they are a second priority (Stratton, 1975; White & Honig, 1995).

Further aggravating the varied challenges to family relations is the police officer's typical reaction to traumatic events. The reaction might surface at home in the form of frustration, anger, grief, confusion, insecurity, disillusionment, or even depression. Family members can become convenient targets of the police officer's misplaced emotions (Kureczka, 1996). As a defense mechanism, many police officers deal with the stress of the job by shutting down emotionally. Detachment and emotional suppression are appropriate while on the job. Self-control may insulate police officers from some of the emotional consequences of the occupation. However, this condition is maintained at a considerable cost. Many police officers are unable to leave their emotions back at headquarters when they go home. For a substantial portion of the workday, police officers must control their emotions. Any show of emotion may make them uncomfortable. In the majority of cases it is this condition that is carried home and the spouse is forced to cope with a non-emotional automaton (Stratton, 1975; Blau, 1994). This emotional withdrawal from family members (diminished communications, inhibited expressions of affection and intimacy) usually results in marital distancing, which further exacerbate stress levels (Hageman, 1978; Blau, 1994; White & Honig, 1995). In some cases the opposite occurs: anger and frustration are displaced at home (Stratton, 1975). The inappropriate displacement of anger can serve to create an environment that places family relationships in greater jeopardy for domestic violence ((White & Honig, 1995). Concurrently, a police officer who is preoccupied with personal problems may become less focused on the job (Clede, 1994). Given the obvious stressors of the job, many spouses feel they cannot discuss family problems because they are concerned about further burdening an already overwhelmed police officer (White & Honig, 1995). Unfortunately, the lack of problem-solving communications serves to prolong discord and family distress. Under such conditions, the underpinnings of any marriage (emotional support, companionship, intimacy), are likely to break down (Alkus & Padesky, 1983).

Considering all of the threats inherent in the occupation, the police officer is more likely to take his or her own life than be killed in the line of duty. As early as 1975, the suicide rate for police officers was found to be considerably higher than the rate of suicides in the general population (Heinman, 1975). The actual suicide rate among police officers may be factually inaccurate due to underreporting as police departments occasionally misidentify a suicide as an accident. Marital discord is the most precipitating stressor and commonly reported factor involved in police officer suicides (Alkus & Padesky, 1983; White & Honig, 1995).

Few occupations demand as much from a family as police work. A strong, well-adjusted family life gives police officers the support they need for performing the considerable, unique, and demanding duties and responsibilities of the job. Considering the obstacles, a good home life is still the best antidote to the stresses of the job (Hall, 1969).

ROLE CONFLICT

Social structures can also create difficult, conflicting, or impossible demands for occupants of such structures (Rommetveit, 1954; Kahn, Wolfe, Quinn, Snoek, & Rosenthal, 1964). Police officers face countless situations in which their roles and responsibilities are unclear (Reiser, 1974a; Teten & Minderman, 1977; Davidson & Vino, 1980; Alkus & Padesky, 1983; Ellison & Genz, 1983; Kroes, 1985; Moyer, 1986; Brown & Campbell, 1994; Van Maaen, 1995). As a result, police officers experience a great deal of internal conflict related to their work.

The actions of police officers affect the lives of others everyday. For example, an arrest may cause the accused to lose their job, pose a serious economic hardship, result in family disgrace, or break-up a marriage. In many situations police officers have the authority to exercise discretion to arrest or not arrest an individual. Exercising either option can be a source of stress for the police officer. Oftentimes this is a "no win" situation given the conflicting societal and departmental expectations for his or her role.

Figure 3.1: Major Roles of a Police Officer

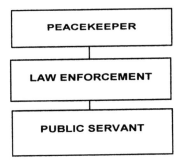

Role ambiguity is another form of role stress and is characterized by vagueness and the lack of agreement regarding role expectations. Role ambiguity results when an employee is unsure as to what type of behavior is appropriate in a given work situation (Robbins & Judge, 2007). Role conflict results when police officers receive incompatible sets of expectations that need to be satisfied simultaneously (Boles, Johnston, & Hair, 1997). Role conflict is a form of role stress in which expectations may be clear, but at the same time contradictory or mutually exclusive (Kahn, et al., 1964).

Identified sources of role stress include the following:

- Lack of clarity regarding the scope of responsibility;
- Vague and inconsistent role expectations;
- Uncertainty regarding whose expectations should be met; and
- Doubts regarding the means used to evaluate role performance (Hardy & Conway, 1978).

Role conflict and role ambiguity exact a price, both in terms of individual well-being and organizational effectiveness. Evidence indicates there is a direct relationship between the degree of role conflict experienced by role occupants and various work-related outcomes such as job-related tension and anxiety, job dissatisfaction, futility, a propensity to resign, lack of confidence in the organization, and the inability to influence decision making (Kahn, et al., 1964; House & Rizzo, 1972; Bedeian & Armenakis, 1981). Conflicting, ambiguous, or unclear goals may underlie increased distress (Pinder, 1984; Luthans, 1985; Violanti & Aron, 1993). Role conflict and ambiguity have been associated with negative effects on both the individuals and organizations involved. Role conflict and ambiguity coupled with the regular exposure to violent events and critical incident traumatic stress can cause police officers to suffer emotionally as well as (Evans, et al., 1992).

Closely related to role conflict and role ambiguity are complications related to the various and sundry occupational demands of the job. Occupational stress is a function of job demands on the worker and his or her ability to control the work (Karasek & Theorell, 1990). Case in point: a police officer must balance the need to apprehend a suspect with the need to protect the suspect's civil rights (Eisenberg, 1975).

The police officer, therefore, must balance the role of peacekeeper and public servant with the role of law enforcement. In addition to their role as "crime busters," police officers must confront forces that are attempting to disrupt social order while at the same time feeling trapped by citizens who demand immediate solutions to problems deeply rooted in the socioeconomic fabric of contemporary society over which they have little or no control (Witkin, et al., 1990).

The police image (being in the public eye: the "fishbowl effect") is also a significant occupational stressor (Bartol, et al., 1992). Arcuri (1977) and Delattre (1989) reported that television programs often portray the police officer as being "superhuman." This representation causes the public to develop unrealistic expectations of police powers. As a result of these unrealistic public expectations, police officers try to live up to their "superman" image, a larger-than-life hero who can do practically anything (Kehr & Prentice, 1981).

The inability to function effectively and deal successfully with people's problems (especially given the constitutional constraints on their authority) confronts police officers everyday (Eisenberg, 1975). When police officers perceive themselves as unable to deal with the demands of the job (that is, live up to their public image), stress is likely to increase (Terry, 1983; Violanti & Marshall, 1983). Police officers also cite erroneous or distorted media coverage of police activities as contributing to the general negative stereotyping of the police, which adds to police officer and family distress (Eisenberg, 1975; Fletcher, 1990; Storch & Panzarella, 1996). Further, inaccurate media reports also result in unfavorable public attitudes, criticism from neighbors, friends, and sometimes family members, all of which cause increased frustration for police officers that can also result in a self-imposed isolation from the mainstream culture, (Van Maanen, 1995; White & Honig, 1995).

The mission of the police fosters a unique subculture. It can be described as a bond that coalesces between individuals under considerable stress, aware of their vulnerability, and on the defensive with the very people they are sworn to protect (Gund & Elliot, 1995).

Bonifacio (1991) reported that it is the police officer's power to protect and punish the citizen that is the catalyst for the public's love-hate relationship with the police. These conditions regularly result in police officers feeling that they are viewed with suspicion and hostility by the people they serve (Evans, et al., 1992).

Research over time has revealed that the perceived public disapproval of the police, more imagined than real, heightens police officer stress levels (Symonds, 1969; Reiser, 1974a; Davidson & Veno, 1980; Alkus & Padesky, 1983; Ellison & Genz, 1983; Stratton, 1984; Kroes, 1985; Stone, 1989; Brown & Campbell, 1990; Prunckun, 1991; More, 1992; Blau, 1994; Van Maanen, 1995; Storch & Panzarella, 1996).

THE CONCEPTION OF JUSTICE

Police officers also report frustration and dissatisfaction with the criminal justice system, particularly the courts, which they perceive inhibit their ability to adequately execute their duties and protect society from criminals. Police officers seemingly continually confront the same offenders over and over again, and are alarmed by the recidivism rate of criminal offenders who seem to be perpetually "on the street," rather than incarcerated (Eisenberg, 1975; Delattre, 1989). In a study of British police officers, Stone (1989) reported the factor perceived as causing the most stress among a sample of the population under study was the apparent leniency of the courts. This condition is often perceived as representing the ultimate futility of the criminal justice system. These constraints frequently impact the police officer's ability to effectively resolve problems encountered on the street and, as a result, fail to satisfy public expectations (Alkus & Padesky, 1983; Terry, 1983; Stratton, 1984; Wilkin, et al., 1990; Stotland, 1991; Bartol, et al., 1992; Evans, et al., 1992; More, 1992; White & Honig, 1995).

Police officers habitually feel betrayed by the criminal justice system. Many court decisions are viewed by the police as undermining their mission. Police officers may find the adversary system difficult to adjust to, particularly when they offer testimony and their honesty and integrity are challenged (Eisenberg,

1975). The police officer may come to distrust the government and its facilities for justice, while at the same time fearing that the elements of turmoil and crime are operating without restriction.

The mechanics of the court system also discourage many police officers. Delays and continuances in the judicial process are perceived as typical of inefficient courtroom management (Eisenberg, 1975). Furthermore, the scheduling of appearances, with rare exception, excludes consideration of a police officer's time and usually interferes with his or her personal lives.

An ancillary component of the criminal justice system is the social service agency. The volume of police work that is non-criminal in nature is substantial, and police-citizen contacts are such that assistance of some sort beyond police intervention is recurrently evident and compelling. However, social service agencies can be a major source of frustration for the police officer. Either there is a lack of referral agencies in a particular jurisdiction or those that do exist are perceived as ineffective. The lack of effectiveness of social service agencies often aggravates police officers who view them as the only source of viable assistance for people in need of help. This can be another cause of stress that contributes to the police officer's overwhelming sense of the inability to contribute significantly to the safety and welfare of those who need public assistance (Eisenberg, 1975).

Before ending the present chapter, a compilation of police stressors developed by Symonds (1969), Stratton (1978) and Luthans (1985) are outlined hereafter:

- Extraorganizational (External)
    1. Society;
    2. Technology;
    3. The family;
    4. Economic and financial conditions;
    5. Race and class;
    6. Community conditions;
    7. The courts and the criminal justice system;
    8. Social service agencies and services;
    9. The public's image of the police;
    10. Negative media coverage; and
    11. Unpopular decisions affecting police work that are made by external administrative agents.
- Group
    1. Cohesiveness;
    2. Social Support;
    3. Conflict; and
    4. Breakdown of relations with peers and supervisors.

- Individual
  1. Type "A" behavior;
  2. Career changes;
  3. Low self-esteem (feelings of inadequacy);
  4. The need for secondary employment; and
  5. Altered status in the community.
- The Job Itself
  1. Shift work/shift schedule;
  2. Boredom;
  3. Work overload;
  4. Role conflict;
  5. Role ambiguity;
  6. Exposure to misery;
  7. Dealing with undesirables;
  8. Handling high-risk/high-threat incidents;
  9. Handling crisis situations;
  10. Exposure to contagious diseases;
  11. Unrealistic public expectations; and
  12. Racial confrontations.

DISCUSSION QUESTIONS

1.   Much has been postulated about what can be done (internally and external-ly) to enhance police officer job satisfaction. Can this sensible objective ever be attained? What are some suggestions that you would recommend to achieve this objective?

2.   Considering the five general categories of police stressors presented at the end of the chapter narrative, which particular stressor under each category would you select as being the most significant cause of stress for a police officer? Briefly explain the reasons for your selections.

3.   In your opinion, what aspect of the job and its related behavior cause the most distress among family members of police officers? Briefly explain your answer. How can this problem be overcome?

4.   How can police camaraderie sometimes be a bad thing? Briefly explain your answer. Don't necessarily limit your selection to the issue of police-family relationships.

CHAPTER FOUR
ORGANIZATIONAL AND INTERPERSONAL STRESSORS

OVERVIEW

Chapter Four is the second segment of a three-part discussion of selected stressors that are caused primarily by the nature of the work itself and by the nature of the police organization. In this chapter, the reader will become familiar with the reasons the organization itself is predictably a major cause of police officer perceived stress.

THE ORGANIZATION

As emphasized throughout the narrative, police officer perceived stress is both an individual and an organizational dilemma (Terry, 1983). Research indicates the most frequently reported source of perceived stress among police officers is workplace frustration—the police department itself (Kroes, Margolis, & Hurrell, 1974b; Jacobi, 1975; Hillgren, Bond, & Jones, 1976; Martinelli, et al., 1989; Crank & Caldero, 1991; Evans, et al., 1992; Hart, et al., 1995; Storch & Panzarella, 1996; Wilson, et al., 1997). Organizational, rather than operational experiences are more important in determining the psychological well-being of police officers (Hart, et al., 1995).

Kohan and Mazmanian (2003) found that organizational experiences are more associated with police officer burnout than operational experiences. Stinchcomb (2004) had similar findings; organizationally-induced stressors have the capacity for taking a far greater toll on the long-term health and well-being of police officers.

Organizational stressors center on work-related conditions including frustration with the police department administration and its policies and procedures (Spielberger, et al., 1981; Kennedy-Ewing, 1989; Hart, et al., 1993; Violanti & Aron, 1995; Storch & Panzarella, 1996). Violanti and Aron (1993) found police organizational stressors increased psychological distress 6.3 times more than inherent police stressors. In 2009, Barath also established that organizational stressors and the administrative practices of the department consistently create the most significant stress for police officers.

The notion that working conditions on the job have an impact on a police officer's level of productivity and their physical and emotional health now seems generally accepted. Research has revealed that certain features of the job contribute to police stress, which includes the following:

- The autocratic-paramilitary and hierarchical organizational structure;
- Inadequate or poor leadership and supervision;
- Excessive paperwork;
- Lack of administrative support;
- Role conflict and ambiguity (unclear expectations);
- Inadequate pay and resources;
- Inadequate communications;
- Adverse work schedules;
- Unfair disciplinary practices;
- Performance evaluations;
- Promotional practices; and
- Lack of recognition and rewards.

(Symonds, 1969; Kroes, et al., 1974b; Jacobi, 1975; Terry, 1975; Hillgren, et al., 1976; Alkus & Padesky, 1983; Wexler & Logan, 1983; Ayres &Flanagan, 1990; Thrash, 1990; Crank & Caldero, 1991; Prunckun, 1991; Stotland, 1991; Moore, 1992; Stinchcomb, 2004). The indicated researchers found one or more of the aforementioned features of the job that contribute to police officer perceived stress in their respective studies.

WORKING CONDITIONS

Inadequate and insufficient equipment and resources are cited by several researchers as contributing to police officer stress (Davidson & Veno, 1980; Wexler & Logan, 1983; Kennedy-Ewing, 1989). One of the most frequent complaints reported by police officers is work overload. That is, being asked to do more with less (Reiser, 1974a; Witkin, et al., 1990). The department's authorized strength and table of organization are rarely filled after retirements causing the remaining police officers to carry inordinate burdens. According to Deeter-Schmelz and Ramsey (1977), work increases as workers face more demands with fewer resources. Budget constraints or the lack of political, public, and administrative support often leave police officers with insufficient or inadequate staffing levels and equipment. Decreased staffing levels and insufficient equipment translates to fewer back-ups, and longer back-up response time.

Other police officer safety issues include the lack of sufficient personnel and essential equipment when it is critically needed (Eisenberg, 1975; Bartol, et al., 1992; White & Honig, 1995).

Like private sector businesses, public sector organizations face the prospect of downsizing. Shaw and Barrett-Power (1997) defined downsizing as a "constellation of stressor events centering around pressures toward workforce reductions, which place demands upon the organization, work groups, and individual employees, and require a process of coping and adaptation" (p. 109). According to Shaw and Barrett-Power, the typical approach organizations use to deal with reduction in force situations is to downsize by layoffs, attrition, redeployment, hiring freezes, or early retirement packages, all of which are perceived by employees as stressful. Lately (2009-10), municipal governments are negotiating contractual "give-backs" that will likely affect pay scales and salaries, healthcare benefits, and retirement benefits while concurrently demanding more production from an already reduced workforce.. Much of the workplace stress results from these discrepancies. There is a gap between what we have (actual conditions) and what is needed to do the job (desired conditions). Demands that are not commensurate with the available resources interfere with organizational objectives and goals, the legal mandates of the police department, and the duties and responsibilities of police officers, which promote stress. Likewise, in many ways these discrepancies determine the overall morale and productivity of the workforce.

RELATIONSHIPS WITH MANAGEMENT

Police officers also list the lack of support from middle and upper level management, and the lack of input into the decisions influencing their work, as significant stressors. Police officers feel they have little or no control or influence over decisions that profoundly affect them (Reiser, 1974a; Jacobi, 1975; Davidson & Veno, 1980; Alkus & Padesky, 1983; Ellison & Genz, 1983; Wexler & Logan, 1983; Stratton, 1984; Evans, et al., 1992; Blau, 1994; Brown & Campbell, 1994; Morash, Haar, & Kwak; 2006). Control seems to be a critical factor in reducing stress on the job. The most serious psychological stressors occur when the demands of the job are high and the employee's control over the work to be performed is low (Karasek & Theorell, 1990). There is considerable more alienation and powerlessness among police officers who have few opportunities to influence policies and procedures. Police officers who have lower levels of participation have been shown to have lower job satisfaction as well (Wagoner, 1976; Morash, et al., 2006).

Police officers are of the opinion that departmental executives are excessive in their attention to detail and in their apparent enthusiasm for fault-finding ("second guessing" and "Monday morning quarterbacking" done by "Chair-borne Commanders"), who offer little in the way of constructive criticism.

These situations can aggravate stress on the job (Kroes, 1985; Ayres & Flanagan, 1990; White & Honig, 1995). Among a sample of police officers, Griggs (1985) found that half of their harmful stressors were caused by the administrative style of their superiors, particularly if the style tends to be autocratic, precluding any chance of active participation in organizational decision making. Following up, Jarmillo, Nixon, and Sams (2005) discovered that job satisfaction, supervisor support, group cohesiveness, and promotional opportunities are the best predictors of organizational commitment on the part of police officers. On the other hand, one of the findings of a study undertaken by Barocas, Canton, Li, and Vlahov (2009) is that job dissatisfaction correlates significantly with perceived stress.

BEHAVIORAL AND PERFORMANCE EXPECTATIONS

Police officers are expected to maintain personal, moral, and professional standards above those that are expected from the general public (Niederhoffer, 1967). The police officer's job performance and conduct are under constant scrutiny by the department, the public, and the media (Stratton, 1975); he or she must face the reality that the department is obligated to establish and enforce performance standards as well as regulate the behavior of its members (Bonifacio, 1991). The department expects its police officers to do everything well. Attempts by police officers to satisfy the performance expectations of the department can produce a stressful overload (Violanti & Aron, 1993). According to Bonifacio (1991), "The policeman [sic] must live with the knowledge that he [sic] will be treated with hostility by the department for failing to live up to its perfectionist demands." (p. 197). Nevertheless, a police officer is likely to make a mistake on occasion and fail to completely satisfy department expectations.

Police officers, particularly those working the street, face many situations in which their actions may be questioned or investigated. If a police officer makes an incorrect judgment (wrong trying to be right), he or she can be second-guessed and subjected to possible sanctions (Alkus & Padesky, 1983; Kroes, 1985; Stone, 1989; Wirkin, et al., 1990). Many department requirements are viewed as threatening or unreasonable (Eisenberg, 1975) and police officers tend to perceive discipline as a rigid, punitive system that is petty (criticizing every error and honest mistake), and unforgiving, with a tendency to overlook positive accomplishments and performance excellence. Recognition for a job well done is rare; criticism for mistakes is frequent (Eisenberg, 1975). The general attitude among police officers is that supervisors and administrators operate to protect and endorse the reputation of the department, but fail to support or demonstrate concern for the individual police officer (Spielberger, et al., 1981; Ellison & Genz, 1983).

REWARDS, RECOGNITION, AND PROMOTIONS

Promotional practices, oftentimes perceived as unfair, along with the lack of promotional opportunities, inadequate rewards, and too little recognition further contribute to stress levels (Reiser, 1974a; Reiser, 1975; Eisenberg, 1975; Davidson & Veno, 1980; Wexler & Logan, 1983; Kennedy-Ewing, 1989; Crank & Caldero, 1991; Bartol, et al., 1992; White & Honig. 1995). On the other hand, recognition and rewards create and maintain high morale (Daniels, 1994; Graves, 1996). Unfortunately, in most departments, there is little opportunity for advancement regardless of the performance of its individual members (Eisenberg, 1975). The lack of self-actualization is fundamental to police alienation (Chandler & Thompson, 1975). Since police officers tend to be very competitive, a long-term failure to receive a promotion may result in feelings of alienation from work groups and are coupled with a sense of individual depression and low self-esteem. For the majority of police officers who are not promoted, the job provides few incentives for self-satisfaction. Consequently, the job may become tedious, especially for police officers who have attained a college education and have high expectations for success and advancement on the job (Graves, 1996). Morale is threatened as police officers perceive a steady decline in the range of career options. Career development is often difficult and the majority of police officers soon realize that finishing their career as basic police officer may be a *fait accompli* (Hurrell, 1986).

GENDER AND MINORITY STRESS

Prior to the 1960s, police departments were staffed predominantly by white males (Darien, 2002). Females and ethnic minorities entering police departments were expected to subordinate themselves to their white male counterparts (Sklansky, 2006). Women were expected to perform their duties and responsibilities the same as male police officers while at the same time retaining their femininity (Darien, 2002).

While police officers who are women experience the same stressors as their male coworkers, there are additional categories of stressors peculiar to police officers who are women. Many of the standard role expectations of a police officer conflict with female role expectations leading to conflicts within herself and with others on and off the job (Alkus & Padesky, 1983). Although they are entering police departments in increasing numbers, women continue to report experiencing stress from working in a male-dominated occupation (Luthans, 1985; Ostrov, 1986; Bartol, et al., 1992). All too often, women lack occupational role models and mentors, and regularly feel excluded from informal channels of support (Morash & Haarr, 1995). In a 1983 study of female police officers, Wexler & Logan found that 80 percent of respondents indicated that they experienced stress from the attitudes of male police officers toward female police officers. "Those most often occurring were questions about the women's sexual orientation, blatant anti-women comments, and the refusal to talk to the women" (p. 48). Sexual innuendos, teasing, and flirting were common occurrences that added to the stress of the job (Weiser-Remington, 1983). These conditions produce a difficult and hostile working environment for women (He, Zhao, & Ren, 2005).

Because they are often viewed in stereotypical ways, women are likely perceived by their male colleagues as being passive, physically weak, and overemotional (Ostrov, 1986). Male police officers typically view female police officers as having a limited role in the department that is separate from the real police work that takes place on the street. Male police officers tend to be overprotective due to a lack of confidence and trust in the abilities of female police officers, thus harming their self-image (Weiser-Remington, 1983). Female police officers have a propensity to avoid seeking assistance from their male colleagues because they do not want to appear weak and incapable of doing the job (Thompson, Kirk, & Brown, 2005). Concomitantly, the uncertainty about the female police officer's ability to do the job is a source of added stress for the male police officers (Logan, 1983). This condition has surely changed in the intervening decades. However, the examples indicate the degree of difficulty experienced by women who entered the police occupation in the not too distant past.

Later research revealed that women are able to do the job of policing at least as well as men. In opposition to the masculine stereotype, women tend to be more service oriented and inclined to resolve issues verbally, rather than physically (Sandler & Mintz, 1974). As a matter of fact, police administrators believe that because female police officers tend to be more empathetic and sensitive, they are able to defuse potentially dangerous situations better than their male colleagues (Martin, 1980; Martin, McKean, & Veltcamp, 1986; Grennan, 1987; Bartol, et al., 1992; Manuel, Retzlaff, Sheehan, 1993, Kay, 1994).

Similar to the experiences of the women mentioned above, ethnic minority members of police departments (both male and female) often experience even greater stress on the job than their white male and white female colleagues. According to Alkus and Padesky (1983), "Minority officers often experience even greater stress than their white, male peers due to hostile stereotypical attitudes" (p. 58). Consequently, minority members may feel the need to work harder and to a higher standard (perhaps approaching perfection) in order to be accepted by their colleagues. These conditions intensify their psychological stress (He, et al., 2005).

EXECUTIVE STRESS

Another group that experiences a unique set of stressors are the police executives. Police officers believe a promotion will alleviate the stress they face everyday. However, once elevated in rank, many find they must contend with a variety of new stressors in addition to the ones they experienced when they were basic police officers (Standfest, 1996). According to Alkus and Padesky (1983), executive stressors are numerous. Police executives face a combination of job stressors that include ambiguous policy direction along with greater responsibilities within the organization. To a large extent, their worth is determined by their ability to negotiate conflicting interests and the capacity to operate in complex political environments (Green & Reed, 1988). Work overload and organizational concerns are prominent among police executives. The executive is faced with complex demands from superiors, subordinates, and the public. The executive may even be pressured by the community to change law enforcement policies over which he or she has little or no control.

Implementing policies and imposing disciplinary sanctions are problematic for police executives particularly when they are opposed by a cohesive group of subordinates. Standfest (1996) reported that in addition to taking disciplinary action against a subordinate, stressors for police executives include making amends with the public because of a subordinate's mistake, a poorly defined role within the department, insufficient support from administrators, little or no input into departmental policy, and authority incommensurate with his or her duties and responsibilities.

The greatest pressure on a police officer comes from superiors in the department who are dependent on his or her performance (Reiser, 1974a). Motivating employees, building morale, performance appraisal, identifying and mitigating personal problems in subordinates, communicating effectively with subordinates, and dealing with staffing shortages and budget constraints are also cited as causes of stress among police executives.

These issues cause the same kinds of stress reactions that a felony-in-progress crime response is likely to provoke among police officers working the street. The consequences of perceived stress can debilitate police executives, which in turn inhibits the effectiveness of the department (Standfest, 1996). Since education has been the cornerstone of the police professionalism movement, police executives with lower levels of education were more likely to perceive stress than the more educated police executives (Craig, Regoli, Hewitt, & Culbertson, 1993). Lower levels of perceived stress were experienced by police executives with post-graduate degrees. This condition has been inter-preted as evidence that educational attainment may provide executives with a buffer against the onset of perceived stress. Further compounding stress for both the police executive and his or her family is that spouses must be cognizant that their behavior will reflect on their police executive spouse (White & Honig, 1995).

SUPERVISOR STRESS

Mid-level supervisors experience much the same kinds of stressors as those ex-perienced by executives. Stress affects supervisors from all sides since they re-ceive pressures from above and below in the organization (Kroes, et al., 1974b). Supervisors not only experience the same stressors experienced by all police officers, but they must also deal with the pressure associated with command. For example, when individuals are promoted, they often must supervise police offic-ers with whom they have developed close working and social relationships. The friendships, and in some cases antagonisms, developed during careers unders-tandably can interfere with a supervisor's ability to impartially perform his or her tasks, which in turn heightens stress levels for both the supervisor and subordinate. According to White and Honig (1995), mid-level managers report frustration with being held accountable for the behavior of their subordinates regardless of whether or not it is feasible to exercise realistic control over them.

Finally, the longer police officers are on the job, the more likely their moti-vation and enthusiasm will decrease (Van Maanen, 1975). The proactive actions, positive attitudes, and the social support offered to police officers by immediate supervisors and department executives have been found to reduce overall stress and improve certain aspects of performance (Deeter-Schmelz & Ramsey, 1997).

DISCUSSION QUESTIONS

1.   What do you consider to be the organization's most significant contribution to police officer perceived stress? Explain your answer. What measures can be taken to stop this from recurring?

2.   Do you believe it is important for police officers to maintain behavioral standards above what is expected from the general public? If so, why? If not, why not?

3.   Why is being promoted from basic police officer to supervisor perceived as being very stressful? What are some of the issues that make it so stressful? Can these issues be effectively resolved? How?

CHAPTER FIVE
INDIVIDUAL STRESSORS

OVERVIEW

Chapter Five is the final segment of a three-part discussion of selected stressors that are caused primarily by the nature of the work itself and by the nature of the police organization. The concluding section identifies several characteristics of the job that generate stress: the realities of the job; assignment workload; work schedule and sleep deprivation; the nature of patrol operations; anxiety; fear; cynicism; responses to major incidents; critical incident stress; emerging issues; and the consequences of cumulative stress. The narrative begins with a brief discussion of the archetypal police officer's distinctive personality.

TYPE "A" PERSONALITY

It is estimated that up to 75 percent of police officers can be categorized as having Type "A" personalities. It is not known, however, whether these traits develop on the job or individuals who posses these traits are attracted to the job (Evans, et al., 1992). What is known is that individuals most susceptible to the adverse influence of stress are those who are anxiety prone and those who are most dedicated to their work (Freudenberger, 1974; Reiser, 1975; Minirth & Meier, 1992). Type "A" personalities operate under almost continuous levels of moderate to high stress (Robbins & Judge, 2007).

Type "A" behavior correlates highly with perceived stress levels and their dangerous physical and psychological consequences. Type "A" personalities are much more prone to the worst outcome of stress—heart attack (Luthans, 1985). Profiles of Type "A" personalities include the following attributes:

- They work long, hard hours under constant deadlines and pressures (real or imagined);
- They often take work home;
- They measures success by quantity;
- They set high standards of productivity that they seem driven to maintain;
- They are obsessed with numbers;
- They are unable to cope with leisure time;
- They are unable to relax;

- They eat rapidly;
- They are constantly in competition with themselves;
- They are often frustrated with the work situation;
- They are competitive;
- They are aggressive;
- They are easily irritated by the work of others;
- They are often misunderstood by their bosses; and
- They are impatient.

(Luthans, 1985; Robbins & Judge, 2007).

Type "A" personalities often exceed performance expectations, which can be advantageous to the organization. However, if not appropriately moderated, these same character traits can harm both the individual and the department.

REALITIES OF THE JOB

Van Maanen (1973), Arcuri (1976), Lefkowitz (1977), Lester (1983), Stratton (1984), and Meagher and Yentes (1986) agree that the first reason articulated by an applicant for wanting to be a police officer is to help the public and assist the powerless and the weak through the lawful exercise of their authority. Police officers feel their work is important to society and they experience great personal satisfaction in helping people in distress. Regardless of their honorable and admirable reasons for wanting to be police officers, they are quick to realize that their work more often than not results in more hostility than admiration (Symonds, 1969; Bonifacio, 1991; Nowicki, 1992).

The world the police officer confronts every day is considerably different than the world any other citizen faces. According to Bonifacio (1991), "The nearly universal experience of policemen [sic] once they hit the street is the staggering amount of misery and degradation that runs rampant there, and the lack of real power they have to do anything about it" (p. 70). The young police officer is quickly socialized to deal with the realities of suffering and death that includes confronting acutely suicidal persons, viewing mutilated homicide victims, and seeing battered children (Alkus & Padesky, 1983). Reiser (1974a) and Bonifacio (1991) reported that the police officer's value system is attacked repeatedly by the degradation they are forced to experience from working the street, and the associated feelings of pain and helplessness. Eisenberg (1975) reported that police officers are constantly exposed to the inequities and brutalities of life that take an emotional toll on even the most well-adjusted police officers. This regular association with suffering causes irreparable emotional harm.

CYNICISM

According to Niederhoffer (1956), "Cynicism is at the very core of police problems" (p. 10). Police officers become increasingly hardened and emotionally detached in the first 18 months on the job (Singleton and Teahan (1978). A police officer who feels his or her work is frustrating, unsatisfying, and unappreciated cannot be expected to maintain discipline or perform the duties and responsibilities of the job enthusiastically (Denyer, et al., 1975). A police officer may soon see the job as demoralizing and worthless, which is a very stressful state to be in for 20 years (Bonifacio, 1991).

For most police officers, the reality of the job soon leads to disillusionment (Symonds, 1969). For example, the police officer must focus on street crime that is often committed by disadvantaged people; yet he or she knows that white collar crime among business and in politics flourishes (Eisenberg, 1975). As a result, police officers soon experience a loss of innocence; idealistic visions of public service may not match the realities of the job, which often cause police officers to lose faith and become cynical over time (Conroy & Hess, 1992; Graves, 1996). Cynicism, which undermines the values needed to accomplish the goals of police work, is particularly high at the level of basic patrol operations where the majority of police officers are assigned (Graves, 1996).

Much of the cynicism derives from the beliefs police officers hold about their perceived lack of community and government support. This cynicism may result because police officers believe the communities they serve want them to fulfill a role without providing them with the support or without authorizing the government to give them adequate legal authority to carry out this role (Evans, et al., 1992). The more cynical their attitudes toward the people they deal with in their work, the more likely they are to be cynical about people in general (Stearns & Moore, 1993). Dyas (1996) wrote

> Among the problems that beset police officers, one concerns the emotional or psychological crisis which seems to come to every active and sincere police officer after a varying number of years of hard work when it all begins to appear useless, a never-ending-going-about-in-circles sort of a job that seems to accomplish nothing. (p. 65).

This condition is a state of mind that can be a precursor to emotional problems, misconduct, brutality, and corruption and it can adversely influence morale and performance and contribute to a diminished quality of life for police officers and their families (Graves, 1996).

WORKLOAD

Gailard and Wientjes (1994) reported that a high workload is regarded as an important although not a critical factor in the development of stress symptoms. These findings were somewhat contradicted later by Williams (2003) who reported that excessive workload and working long hours invariably leads to higher stress levels for police officers. Collins and Gibbs reported similar findings in 2003.

Research has confirmed that the type of assignment can influence police officer pessimism. In a study of attitudes concerning their role in the community, Brooks, et al. (1994) learned that police officers assigned to work in so-called "quiet" geographic areas tend to see their community more optimistically than their counterparts who work in busier geographic areas. Police officers assigned to less busy geographic areas, which are more service oriented, believe that the citizens who reside there support them more. Conversely, police officers who work in busy, high crime areas believe that the residents are hostile to the police and abhor their very presence in the neighborhoods. As a result, police officers assigned to these sectors may well have a negative impression of both the citizens and the job itself.

WORK SCHEDULE AND SLEEP DEPRIVATION

Rotating work shifts and the rigors of constantly having to adapt to changing sleeping and eating habits are reported to be significant stressors (Eisenberg, 1975; Kroes, 1985; Blau, 1994; Storch & Panzarella, 1996). Shift work has been shown to have an adverse impact on physical health and the ability to perform the duties and responsibilities of the job at maximum efficiency (Kroes, 1976; Stone, 1989; Stotland, 1991; Moore, 1992). What is more, Williams (2003) found that rotating shift workers are more likely to have accidents or be injured on the job.

The health consequences of shift work can be seen in circadian factors, disturbed sleep patterns, and cardiovascular disease (O'Neill & Cushing, 1991). A worker on a rotating shift is unable to satisfactorily adjust his or her body clock before it is time to readjust.

This practice alone is one of the primary stressors among emergency service workers (Mitchell & Resnick, 1981; Kennedy-Ewing, 1989; Pierson, 1989; Mitchell & Everly, 1993). Because rotating shifts are inherently detrimental, they should be kept to a minimum (Vila, 2009).

According to Dr. William C. Dement (1976), one of the nation's leading researchers on the subject of sleep, all creatures are influenced by the endless succession of the day and night as the rotation of the earth imposes its daily cycle on all of us. "Night follows day, day follows night, and even if we don't sleep, the sleep-wakefulness rhythm continues in the form of a profound fluctuation in sleepiness and alertness" (pp. 16-18). Vila (2009) found that sleep-loss related fatigue degrades police officer performance and productivity, as well as their health, well-being, and safety.

The negative influences of sleep deprivation that are associated with rotating shifts range from gastrointestinal disorders and elevated serum cholesterol levels to nutritional deficiencies and psychomotor difficulties (Reintzell, 1990). An irregular shift schedule also has an adverse impact on social planning, recreational and relaxation regimens, and the quantity and quality of sleep. All of these maladies typically result in an inferior work product and changes in mood (Stone, 1989; White & Honig, 1995).

THE NATURE OF PATROL OPERATIONS

A large percentage of police work on the street is of a sedentary nature (Kehr & Prentice, 1981), with most calls for service unrelated to criminal activity. Service provided by basic patrol operations that are not directly connected to incidents of crime or suspicious activities make up the large majority of calls for service (Teten & Mindermann, 1977). As a result, police officers must deal with an unusual combination of boredom followed by moments of extreme arousal; from mundane, routine tasks to the occasional life threatening situation. The police officer is always on view, exposed to danger and the unknown. This state of tension (high alert status) is a constant strain on the police officer.

Violence and danger are omnipresent and are threats to police officer safety. Complacency kills. They must approach every incident expecting violence (Symonds, 1969; Teten & Mindermann, 1977; Brown, 1981; Wexler & Logan, 1983; White & Honig, 1995).

A police officer on routine patrol who suddenly must respond to an emergency is in a very stressful situation in which the fight-or-flight response is automatically triggered. That innate instinct, which served as a survival reaction can add to the existing hazards of police work unless managed effectively (Westmoreland & Haddock, 1989). This indispensable condition causes the police officer to be in a constant state of hypervigilence while on the job, and can put the nervous system into overdrive (Alkus & Padesky, 1983; Gilmartin, 1986). The condition of alert preparedness for the eventuality of dealing with a potentially life threatening matter influences the totality of the police officer's role performance. The intensity of this small segment of the job experience is so great that it dominates the police officer's approach to dealing with people.

As specified above, at almost any time a quick response to a particular situation may be required and such a response is jolting to the police officer's physical and mental state (Eisenberg, 1975). Emergency driving, for example, is very stressful. When a police officer responds to an emergency call, his or her heart rate will increase dramatically from the increased adrenalin. It is also tantamount to activation of the fight-or-flight response. The brain slows its processes and is able to handle only essential functions (Westmoreland & Haddock, 1989). Stress and fatigue can lead to accidents especially when attention, judgment, and coordination are narrowly focused (Kottage, 1992; Howard & Joint, 1994). The police officer's stress is really his or her feelings of distress in trying to continuously cope with anxiety-provoking events (Graham-Bonnalie, 1972). According to Alkus & Padesky (1983), "anxiety is experienced as nervousness or edginess, accompanied by rapid mood changes and a quick defensive posture" (p. 59). However, the police officer must deny and overcome emotional reactions while at the same time presenting an image of power and control (Witkin, et al., 1990; Bonifacio, 1991).

FEAR

Dangerous and fearful events occur continually in police work, and police officers may suffer from continuous exposure to fear (Eisenberg, 1975; Wexler & Logan, 1983; Stone, 1989; Mattison, 1990; Stotland, 1991). When improperly managed, fear distorts perceptions, and exaggerates and strains one's stereotypes and prejudices. These suspicions include racial fear, cultural fear, fear of being physically harmed, psychological fear, and the fear of peer disapproval (McCarthy, 1990). Since a police officer has no way of knowing the true danger of a situation beforehand, he or she must approach all calls with caution ("vulnerability awareness" [Solomon, 1990]). These experiences may modify a police officer's personality so as to make him or her less able to perform a major part of the job—service to people—without some abrasiveness and conflict that is oftentimes attributable to fear. Solomon (1990a) and McCarthy (1990) defined fear as an automatic emotional reaction to a perceived danger or threat. It is an alarm response characterized by a high negative affect and arousal. According to McCarthy, unreasonable fear provokes an unreasonable response on the part of the police officer. Fear that is unwarranted creates the same emotional reaction to perceived danger and is likely to generate a negative response simply because the reaction to what is happening is unjustified. There are several fears that influence the police officer's psychological and emotional reactions that can be categorized as unreasonable. Unreasonable fear as defined by McCarthy is "any fear generated in the officer's mind that has no direct correlation with the facts or the situation at hand" (p. 23). Unreasonable fear can cause a police officer to respond to a situation inappropriately. That is, the perceived threat is not real. Simply stated, the police officer perceived a threat when there was none.

The effects of fear may be the result of the individual being unable to adjust quickly enough to the suddenness of stress (Graham-Bonnalie, 1972). Regardless, police officers are expected to immediately overcome their fear and respond appropriately to any contingency.

According to Janik (1990), inhibiting the admission of fear is the anxiety that disclosure will stigmatize the police officer making him or her appear to be weak in the eyes of fellow police officers and, therefore, incapable of taking charge in a given situation. The repression of this emotion in and of itself is a stressor. It is important to add that fear in dangerous situations can be controlled to the point where it does not cause impropriety or inaction on the part of the police officer. Furthermore, fear can be used constructively to motivate police officers to learn from past experience, to improve their conduct, and to develop habitual coping responses to danger. Fear cues police officers to stay alert and mobilize for action (Solomon, 1990). Because policing is dangerous occupation, the reality is that extremely fearful events occur continuously. A police officer may be surprised *when* an incident occurs, but cannot be surprised *that* it happens (Mattison, 1990). Thus, the goal of eliminating fear is both unreasonable and undesirable. It simply must be managed properly.

Figure 5.1: Selected Solutions for Coping with Fear (McCarthy, 1990).

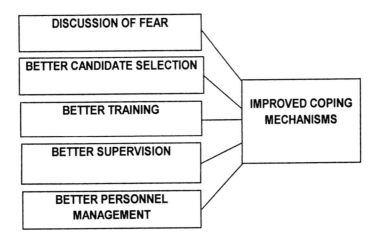

PERFORMANCE EXPECTATIONS DURING EMERGENCIES

Police officers are faced with a myriad of emergency responses that require decision-making and discipline under the most adverse and stressful conditions. Nevertheless, they are expected to maintain self-control and perform their duties competently and effectively. Emotional involvement must be avoided (Larsson & Starrin, 1988). Emotional detachment must occur at the scene or the police officer's job cannot be accomplished. According to Violanti and Marshall (1983), "Police occupational norms view depersonalization as necessary for effective police work" (p. 393). Pogrebin and Poole (1992) reported that the public expects the police to handle critical incidents in a calm, fearless, reassuring, and objective manner. "Police officers are expected to maintain a poised presence even under the most tragic circumstances. Their authority and effectiveness in handling such events would be compromised if officers could not control their emotions" (p. 397). In short, while an emergency may temporarily overwhelm a police officer's coping mechanisms, he or she must adjust quickly and take control of themselves as well as the situation.

CRITICAL INCIDENT STRESS

Most early studies of trauma stress in policing are focused almost exclusively on post-shooting incidents. Later research encompasses the stress induced by other traumatic events collectively referred to as critical incident stress or post-traumatic stress. Critical incidents are sudden, powerful, and perhaps overwhelming events outside of the range of ordinary human experience. According to Mitchell (1983), "Critical incidents produce a characteristic set of psychological and physiological reactions or symptoms in all people" (p. 36). The critical incident stress syndrome is defined as a normal person suffering from a reaction to an abnormal event. Critical incident stress, which tends to be sudden and unexpected, is perhaps the most obvious operational stressor in policing.

Critical incident stress has the potential to impose a profound toll on the average police officer (Resier & Geiger, 1984; Bryant, 1990; Reese, Horn, & Dunning, 1991; Mitchell & Everly, 1993). These incidents can inflict mental harm just as much as they can cause physical wounds (Kreskas, 1996).

Police officers, because of their repeated exposure to scenes of carnage and mayhem, are at risk for the onset of emotional distress. Emotional symptoms that develop as part of the stress response are normal. However, the symptoms have the potential to become dangerous if they are prolonged. The highest levels of stress occur immediately prior to or during the critical incident (Anderson, Litzenberger, & Plecas, 2002). Symptoms typically subside in a matter of weeks although a few of those affected will suffer permanent emotional distress that will adversely affect their continued value to the police department and cause problems in their personal lives as well (Pierson, 1989).

Incidents that are known to have a significant impact on emergency service workers include the following:

- The serious injury or death of a coworker, particularly in the line of duty;
- The suicide or the unexpected death of a coworker;
- The serious injury or death to a civilian, particularly a child;
- The loss of a victim after a prolonged rescue attempt;
- An incident that attracts unusually excessive media coverage;
- Any incident charged with profound emotion;
- A multi-casualty incident;
- A barricaded person/hostage incident; and
- A personal identification with the victim or circumstance.

These incidents, while intrinsic to the job, typically are beyond the realm of normal human experience.

To assume that emergency service workers are somehow desensitized to human tragedy is erroneous (Mitchell & Resnick, 1981; Kennedy-Ewing, 1989; Pierson, 1989; Mitchell & Everly, 1993; Kureczka, 1996). As in many stressful events, social support from colleagues during the incident is a significant protective factor (Martin, M., Marchand, Boyer & Martin, N., (2009).

Multi-casualty incidents such as civil disorders, acts of terrorism, accidents, or fires are powerful events that can initiate a broad spectrum of psychological reactions in emergency service workers. These sudden, violent, intense, threatening, and devastating events have consequences that reach beyond the scene of the emergency and produce serious emotional turmoil for those who encounter them (Mitchell, 1986a). Selye (1956) characterized trauma under the rubric of "catastrophes" that have a stressor effect of "apprehensive avoidance, stunned immobility, apathy, depression, docile dependency, and aggressive irritability" (p. 392). Mitchell (1986a) reported that the first stress reactions to a critical incident include anxiety, shock, fear, disorganization, terror, and occasionally panic. Bohl (1995) reported that immediate responses to a critical incident are physiological and can include muscle tremors, nausea, hyperventilation, faintness, sweating, and perceptual distortions. These maladies are followed within minutes or hours of the episode by shock, fear, denial, anger, numbing, and a general feeling of unreality. At the outset of the incident, the police officer quickly realizes he or she is not in control of the situation. At this interval, the police officer must face the reality of his or her vulnerability and lack of control, and he or she may feel weak and helpless as a result.

During a critical incident, fear, according to Solomon (1990a), can over-whelm a police officer's ability to function appropriately if he or she remains focused solely on the threatening and overwhelming aspects of the situation. According to Alkus and Padesky (1983), "The police officer, given his or her specific pyscho-social role, is not free to fight back, display fear and anger, or run away" (p. 58).

Immediately after this vulnerability awareness phase passes, the reality of the threat must be acknowledged without further delay. According to Mitchell (1987b), if the stressful event does not begin to subside, the reactions to stress may disrupt the police officer's abilities so seriously they can become partially or fully dysfunctional at the scene. At this juncture the police officer must begin to comprehend and make sense out of what is happening and try to gain control of the situation. The police officer must quickly realize something must be done if the challenge is to be met. Solomon (1990a) reported that only when the police officer effectively transitions from the emotional impasse and the feelings of helplessness to effective cognitive and physical action, can the incident be managed to a favorable outcome.

As previously indicated, exposure to a critical incident requires the police officer to make extraordinary emotional adjustments. Mitchell (1987b) indicated that the effects of stress creep up on police officers who are intensely involved in the operations at the scene of the emergency. Bohl (1995) reported that a critical or traumatic event produces sufficient emotional power to overcome the usual coping abilities of an individual. According to Bonifacio (1991), during a critical incident the police officer feels overwhelmed and his or her feelings of omnipotence and invulnerability are shattered by the stressful experience. In many cases, there are aftershocks in which police officers exposed to traumatic events experience feelings of anger at what happened along with feelings of helplessness and frustration that not enough was done. Some police officers suffer a sense of grief, anger, or even fear of a like-event reoccurring. Once over, it is not uncommon for police officers to suffer from nightmares or flashbacks (Palahunic, McCafferty, & Domingo, 19889; Evans, et al., 1992). Poor eating and sleeping habits may also result along with moodiness, irritability, and anxiety. One of the worst problems is the reliving of the event over and over and being excessively self-critical.

Figure 5.2: Five Phases of a Crisis (Mitchell & Resnick, 1981).

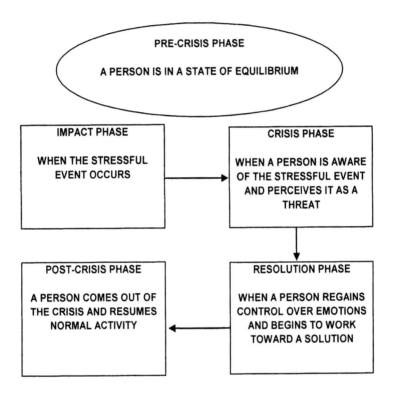

COMBAT TRAUMA

Combat trauma is another aspect of critical incident stress. In the case of a combat situation the police officer must not only be terrified of the deadly force encounter, but also apprehensive of the departmental ramifications he or she may subsequently face (Paul, 1990). According to Finn and Tomz (1997), the stress of this particular type of critical incident is commonly compounded by the ensuing investigation, during which the police officer may feel second-guessed and/or considered guilty of wrongdoing by his or her superiors, the media, and the public. Following a shooting incident involving death or serious injury, the police officer may endure severe emotional distress. This distress can be exacerbated when a police officer's gun is taken away after a deadly force incident. The impact varies with each individual. In some cases there is no observable change; in others it may reveal itself within hours or days. According to Stratton

(1984), Kroes (1985), Mantell (1986), Wittrup (1986), and Saathoff and Buchman (1990), disbelief, anger, fear, guilt, shame, elation, loss of patience, preoccupation with the incident, sadness and depression, feelings of helplessness, nightmares, flashbacks, and insomnia may follow. One may even want to immediately resign from the department (Clede, 1994).

Police officers who encounter violence may develop debilitating defense mechanisms as well (Anderson & Bauer, 1987). Classic signs include reliving the event, loss of interest in life, detachment from others, guilt, and becoming inattentive and forgetful. In some cases, even basic obligations such as reporting for work can be very stressful (Curry, 1995). According to Machel (1993), "Without treatment, these symptoms will psychically reinforce the initial trauma of the person. It is an emotional process which feeds on itself; growing, deepening, ingraining itself over time if not interrupted" (p. 25).

HOSTAGE AND BARRICADED PERSONS

According to Bohl (1995), stress symptoms in police officers can occur after a variety of traumatic experiences, of which a police officer-involved shooting is only one. Police officers involved in hostage negotiations and barricaded situations, for example, typically experience high levels of stress. Hostage negotiators often experience pressure to end the negotiations. Lives, however, depend on whether or not the negotiator can successfully defuse a dangerous situation. They must remain calm and in control even when others behave emotionally. The most intense form of internal stress comes from the negotiator's fear that the incident will escalate.

If negotiations fail to end successfully, the negotiator may feel considerable guilt, anger, and depression particularly if the incident results in the death of the hostage taker and/or the hostages, or the serious injury or death of a police officer. An event of this magnitude is usually handled by a specially trained special operations team consisting of highly skilled police personnel. Even so, the unique pressures, conflicts, and frustrations associated with the incident may affect even the best trained and emotionally stable police officers, either at the seen or some time afterward (Pierson, 1989). If negotiators or special weapon team members fail to acknowledge their feelings, classic post-traumatic stress symptoms are likely to result (Bohl, 1992).

CONSEQUENCES OF CUMULATIVE STRESS

Because traumatic events are outside the realm of normal human experience, they can be expected to cause significant emotional reactions. Reactions may occur as a result of a single event or an accumulation of events. Rivers (1993) labeled this condition, "sequential traumatization." Constant exposure to traumatic incidents renders the police officer particularly vulnerable to the effects of sequential traumatization. According to Beaton and Murphy (1992), the cumulative effects of repetitive exposure to traumatic events can threaten the health and safety of the police officer. The cumulative effects of critical incident stress can exact a growing toll. Each person has a unique reaction to stress. One individual may be greatly affected by a particular incident. Some may even suffer permanent emotional trauma. Others may appear completely unaffected. Some police officers may begin to have spousal and family problems, instigate incidents of excessive force on the job, start abusing alcohol and drugs, and begin to suffer from depression or ulcers, all of which are symptoms of trauma-related stress (Clede, 1994). Some police officers may go on about their lives as though nothing particularly stress-provoking had occurred. Nevertheless, critical incidents are very disturbing and typically challenge an individual's capacity to cope and may become a substantial threat to their psychological and physical well-being (River, 1993).

The police officer who is experiencing significant stress and unable to cope may create a circumstance in which he or she becomes the focus of sympathy, care, and concern. This can even lead to a situation in which the police officer is the source of his or her own injury. The dynamic is similar to that of a suicide gesture (DiVasto & Saxton, 1992). Alcoholism is a major problem among police officers seeking relief from stress (Luthans, 1985; Bryant, 1990; Graves, 1996). In fact, because of stress-related problems, police officers are more likely to become alcohol and drug dependent than the general population (Beuter, Nussbaum, & Meredith, 1988). Alcohol and drugs are an escape into the euphoria of fantasy for the police officer, rather than facing the problems of reality (Graham-Bonnalie, 1972). Drinking is a form of "numbing-out" (Dietrich & Smith, 1986; Winthrop 1986). According to Bonifacio (1991), "The major symptoms described in the police psychology literature are alcohol abuse, marital problems, and thoughts of suicide" (p. 162).

Exposure to a traumatic event increases the risks of Post- traumatic Stress Disorder symptoms, which can lead to alcohol and suicide ideation (Violanti, 2004). Therefore, employers, according to McFarlane and Bryant (2007), are obliged to have an active strategy in place to anticipate and manage the aftermath of a police officer's exposure to traumatic stressors. Rapid and effective assessment and intervention strategies devised to mitigate the impact of the event are necessary to prevent long-term aftereffects, and to accelerate the healing process (Mitchell, 1986a).

Symptoms of post-traumatic stress include the following:

- Cognitive
    1. Confusion in thinking;
    2. Difficulty making decisions;
    3. Lowered concentration;
    4. Memory dysfunction; and
    5. Lowering of all higher cognitive functions.
- Physical
    1. Extensive sweating;
    2. Dizzy spells;
    3. Increased heart rate;
    4. Elevated blood pressure; and
    5. Rapid breathing.
- Emotional
    1. Emotional shock;
    2. Anger;
    3. Grief;
    4. Depression; and
    5. Feeling overwhelmed.
- Behavioral
    1. Changes in ordinary behavior patterns;
    2. Changes in eating habits;
    3. Decreased personal hygiene;
    4. Withdrawal from others; and
    5. Prolonged silence. (Mitchell & Everly, 1993).

High risk factors for the onset of Post-traumatic Stress Disorder (PTSD) include the consequences associated with cumulative stress. Weiss (2002) learned that routine, repetitive job stressors significantly increase a police officer's risk for experiencing PTSD symptoms, rather than the number or severity of the traumatic events they experience. Further, Haisch and Meyers (2004) found that high levels of work-related stress places police officers at a greater risk for being subjected to the symptoms of PTSD.

EMERGING ISSUES

The necessity of having to learn new computer skills is an up-and-coming issue that is increasing police officer perceived stress (Williams, 2003). Recently, several police officers have begun reporting that this added stressor is becoming more apparent each day. New pressure and anxiety is being experienced since the innovative advances in information technology have become a part of the police officer's everyday routine. It is expected that the most senior members of the department will have some difficulty adjusting to the use of computers for information input and retrieval and report writing. Apprehension, however, is not limited to senior police officers. Even the computer literate generation is experiencing frustration with the technology. Computer failures and breakdowns are causing delays in generating and receiving information as well as delays in report preparation and submission of the reports in a timely manner. Too often computer failures result in "missing" data from the field. Police officers also report delays in returning to an in-service/available status because the system is rejecting reports submitted from their radio patrol car computers. The transition from a paper to a paperless system has by no means eradicated the stressors associated with "paperwork."

Computer-related difficulties are not limited to the radio patrol car console. If the in-car computer is not working properly, the user must generate the report from a terminal at police headquarters. Since it may not be possible to do so immediately, the delay may result in the report being submitted at the end of the tour. All too often, the report lacks the detail it would typically have if it had been prepared without delay after the investigation was conducted on the street. Delays also result in police officers remaining at work beyond the end-of-tour time necessitating costly and unwanted overtime.

There is also one interesting consequence of information technology that perhaps was unforeseen. That is, less eye contact with supervisors. This results in less conversation between supervisor and subordinate during which advice and constructive criticism can be offered.

Another unintended outcome is a diminution of the interpersonal relationship that is essential between the members of a squad of police officers and their supervisors. Electronic "conversation" in the form of e-mails transmitted between police officers and their supervisors has become a substitute for face-to-face verbal interaction. Even certain radio calls are received electronically, rather than over the police radio.

There are dangers associated with the electronic exchange of information between the police officer inside of the radio patrol car and outside agents—distraction. A police officer's attention becomes focused on the computer screen instead of what is happening outside of the radio patrol car where an imminent threat may exist. Hopefully, voice-activated commands will someday replace the finger-to-keyboard strokes and lessen the diversion.

During the Scientific Management period in the United States (1856–1915) machines were new and innovative inventions, and man was considered an extension of the machine. Are we now becoming an extension of the computer? These emerging issues must be carefully examined to learn to what extent they are contributing to police officer stress.

DISCUSSION QUESTIONS

1. What character traits of a Type "A" personality can be a benefit to the department? Give an example of how each character trait you selected can benefit the department.

2. What character traits of a Type "A" personality can potentially harm the department? Give an example of how each character trait you selected can harm the department.

3. Do you think that cynicism is an evolving phenomenon of the job, or is there something specific that can occur to cause its abrupt onset? What would have to happen for this condition to take place suddenly?

4. In your opinion, which individual stressor is likely to have the most severe cumulative impact on a police officer? Why?

5. Briefly illustrate a catastrophic scenario unique to the police occupation that is most likely to cause a police officer to suffer from long-term consequences of traumatic stress.

6. Cumulative stressors can result in significant functional failures for those who are repeatedly exposed to stressful situations. Delineate the typical functional failures and include a set of real-world examples for each consequence in your answer.

CHAPTER SIX
PERCEIVED STRESS AND LENGTH OF SERVICE

OVERVIEW

In the present chapter, the reader will learn the reasons why the relationship between perceived stress and length of service is an important consideration in the study of police officer stress. Perceived stress is the degree to which individuals interpret experiences that are stressful to themselves (Brown & Campbell, 1990). Research has revealed that police officers pass through transitory or longitudinal stages during their careers, which may influence the police officer's perception of stress (Neiderhoffer, 1967; Violanti, 1993). It is important to establish at what stage in a police officer's career he or she will experience the highest levels of perceived stress. In doing so, information will be made known that can influence decisions about police training programs as well as time-sensitive instruction and counseling initiatives. Each career stage represents a unique opportunity for the mitigation of police officer perceived stress.

STAGES OF A POLICE OFFICER'S CAREER

Perceived stress in the police occupation appears to run a predictable course highly dependent on length of service and the job environment.

Evans, et al. (1992) offered support for arguments advanced in the police literature that police officers show differing behavior patterns over their periods of service confirming that there are subtle differences between groups of police officers with different lengths of service. Rafsky, Lawley, and Ingram (1976), Violanti (1983), Patterson (1992), and Boyd (1994) asserted that tenure may be a factor in how a police officer reacts to perceived stress at each phase of his or her career. Because these studies propose that time transitions in police careers may alter one's perception of stress, the importance of establishing milestones in the careers of police officers is an important factor in determining when perceived stress levels are the highest. Accordingly, researchers have classified the stages of a police officer's career as represented in the following diagram:

Figure 6.1: Stages of a Police Officer's Career.

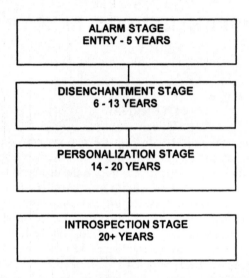

According to Neiderhoffer (1967) and Violanti (1983), in the Alarm Stage, the entry level police officer realizes that police work in the real world is somewhat different from what is learned in the police academy. Perceived stress is likely to be considerable during the Alarm Stage as the "rookie" police officer is exposed to "reality shock" and begins to experience scenes while working the street that include pain, suffering, and the deaths of crime and accident victims. The Disenchantment Stage is an extension of the "reality shock" experienced during the first five years on the job. According to Violanti (1983), "Idealistic notions fostered in the police academy become further and further apart from reality during this stage" (p. 212). During this period, police officers tend to realize that the duties and responsibilities of the job outweigh their ability to successfully cope with the demands and pressures; they begin to develop a sense of personal failure and helplessness in seemingly having no real positive influence on crime control and the quality of life of the people they are sworn to serve and protect. Researchers determined that police officer perceived stress was highest in the Disenchantment Stage (Violanti, 1983; Violanti & Marshall, 1983; Burke, 1989; Patterson, 1992; Boyd, 1994).

Perceptions of the job begin to change at mid-career. During the Personalization Stage, police officers begin to evaluate their intentions and capabilities; failure at police tasks is less important to them than in earlier years, and the demands of policing become less important. This condition contributes to a reduction in perceived stress levels. Finally, police officers nearing the end of their careers see it as a time of reflection as they approach retirement. The

Introspection Stage is a time of relative security for police officers as they tend to worry even less about the demands and failures of the job. It is perhaps the least stressful period in the career of a police officer. If a stage in a police officer's career can be identified as particularly stressful, police departments will be in a better position to proactively assist police officers as they approach a specific transitory stage.

Should there be a relationship between perceived stress and length of service, the necessary and appropriate coping mechanisms can be engaged before the consequences of stress can harm the individual, the organization, and society.

SYNOPSIS OF THE 1999 LONGITUDINAL STUDY

A study of municipal police officers working in three New Jersey counties (Atlantic, Burlington, and Camden) was conducted in 1999 (Daniello). The research questions explored in the study were as follows:

1. Is perceived stress in the police occupation a constant factor?
2. Is it possible that police perceptions of stress change after a continued exposure to police work?

These questions were examined by tracing perceived stress levels through longitudinal stages of a police career. The research assumed that perceived stress among police officers is a phenomenon that exists across the entire population of police officers and can be measured using a validated survey instrument (Langner, 1962). The 1999 study further assumed that police officers throughout the State of New Jersey have been exposed to essentially the same stressors that are routinely experienced by police officers throughout the United States. The results differed from previous research.

Although the present study reached a similar conclusion that perceived stress is not a constant factor, unlike the previous findings, the highest perceived stress levels did not occur during the Disenchantment Stage of a police officer's career. The present study revealed that perceived stress levels tended to be higher at the beginning of a police career, in the Alarm Stage. The 1999 findings indicate that while perceived stress levels are relatively high at the outset of a police career, they tend to diminish over time, suggesting that work experience may moderate police officer reactions to stressful situations.

They also imply that despite the pressures of the occupation police officers manage to cope with the causes and consequences of perceived stress by perpetually adjusting to stressful conditions. The findings of the 1999 study are important because they demonstrate that the course of perceived stress may be changing, and that stress reduction initiatives ought to be concentrated during the Alarm Stage period.

PERCEIVED STRESS IN THE ALARM STAGE

Many stressors that are experienced in the early phase of a police career may be the result of overwhelming or unrealistic job expectations. There are a number of conditions occurring during the Alarm Stage that may contribute to higher perceived stress levels. These stressors commence as an individual makes the transition from civilian to police officer and are collectively regarded as first-time experiences. One reason young people in particular choose a career as a police officer is for an altruistic reason—to serve society. When confronted with an unexpectedly hostile or indifferent public, idealistic police officers feel betrayed. During this period of his or her career, the police officer quickly learns that the idealism of the academy does not necessarily reflect the reality of the job. Life on the mean streets is exactly what the expression implies. They quickly believe their world has changed forever.

The real world of policing demands maximum responsibility while at the same time providing minimum control over the situations in which the police officer becomes involved. This in and of itself can be a major cause of stress at the outset of police career. The portrayal of the police officer as an invincible warrior is a poor match with the realities of life on the beat.

Until the individual learns appropriate and necessary coping methods, this condition too can be overwhelming. All of this suggests that the reality of the streets often shock police officers who are fresh out of the academy. This is a time when they may see themselves as the guardians of a community's peace and safety, an awesome responsibility. During this early stage the individual sees, perhaps for the first time, the "bad" part of society. This may skew his or her opinion as to the character of all people. It begins to create a jaundiced and critical view of the world, and provokes an "us against them" attitude about society. It may be correspondingly difficult to trust a fellow human being (who is not a police officer) when so much of the day is spent dealing with people who are perceived as untrustworthy. This lack of trust can manifest itself in the way a police officer deals with people on a personal level such as neighbors, relatives, friends, and family. Police officers are seen as authority figures and people deal with them differently, even when they are not working. When a problem occurs, everyone looks to the police to "take charge" and solve the problems. This Action Imperative Syndrome (Do something!) can be overwhelming in part because of the lack of experience on the job.

Wearing the uniform makes them separate from the society they serve. This segregation may cause some initial psychological consequences as they experience this isolation for the first time in their lives. They often face overt hostility. For the first time they sense the very image they project causes apprehension and resentment among people they are sworn to protect. At this interval, the police officer may distance him/herself from family and friends and withdraw from society. He or she may fall into a state of confusion, apathy, and frustration. Police officers who happen to belong to minority groups often experience the added aggravation of feeling alienated from other members of their minority group for the first time.

Police occupational norms view depersonalization as necessary for effective police work. A good police officer is expected to show no emotion. This depersonalization creates an incongruity between institutionally demanded and actual human emotions.

This condition is actually forced onto the police officer at the outset of their careers and often leads to an immediate increase in stress. The depersonalization process also limits the freedom of expression the police officer enjoyed as a civilian.

Individuals, perhaps for the first time, must control their emotions. They learn as a police officer that they must be calm and under control, constantly guarding their emotions. They learn that emotions such as anger, disgust, and sadness must not be displayed if they are to maintain a professional image and gain the trust and respect of their peers. Their ability to deal directly with emotional stress, strain, and anxiety is highly circumscribed. While emotional suppression may serve to achieve occupationally functional objectives, this condition may be particularly intrinsically stressful during the early stages of employment as the new officer tries to learn the job and live up to the department's expectation as well as the expectations of fellow officers and the public.

Police work frequently requires police officers to make instantaneous decisions. There is little or no time to mentally rehearse for potentially stressful events when they typically present themselves without warning. Police activity can shift quickly from passivity to frenzy and unexpected danger. Police officers go from one unpredictable situation to another. Individuals may experience for the first time a different kind of stress as they go from complete calm or boredom to a high state of stress without forewarning. This "burst" of stress can cause an inexperienced police officer to perceive a situation as being out of control before he or she can adapt to it. There is a need to be in constant emotional control as the job demands extreme restraint under highly emotional circumstances. As stated previously, this forced-control condition can be overwhelming, particularly during the early years of a police career as the individual is expected to mask emotions perhaps for the first time.

Along with the necessity for composure during high-stress events, a successful police career requires excellent discretionary skills and good judgment.

In the early phase of a career, the police officer may not yet posses the requisite skills to handle decision making situations that necessitate discretion and sound reasoning. The proficiencies associated with good judgment are typically acquired over time and learned through experience. If an entry-level police officer has limited social skills, having to talk to people and try to reconcile issues and resolve disputes during a tour of duty could be especially stressful.

Authoritarianism is a behavioral trait that is considered necessary by police organizations. Police perform their duties in a quasi-military, structured institution. Many individuals entering police departments have no military experience. Consequently, the transition from civilian to police officer initially may be overwhelming given the demands for conformity and discipline. Even the police academy regimen can be a form of "culture shock" if the recruit has never experienced military boot camp training. During the early years of a career, individuals may perceive this process and the related behavioral expectations as dehumanizing.

Individuals may be experiencing shift work (the rotating shift) for the first time. This condition of employment introduces the police officer to a new and unusual life style; one that is in opposition to the circadian clock stability to which they were accustomed. It may upset the physical and mental balance as well as the routine patterns that are needed to ensure successful relationships, including marriage and family development.

The candidate selection process, police academy regimen, field training, and department performance standards and behavioral expectations may account for a higher level of perceived stress among police officers in the Alarm Stage as they try to "make it" in their new career. Police officers who participated in the 1999 study reported higher perceived stress levels at the outset of their respective careers. In many instances the "system" was the basis for elevated perceived stress levels among police officers during their first five years of service as they make the difficult transition from civilian to police officer. They soon realize that becoming a police officer involves not only a career change, but a lifestyle change as well.

Figure 6.2: The "Entry System" (Typically entry to two years).

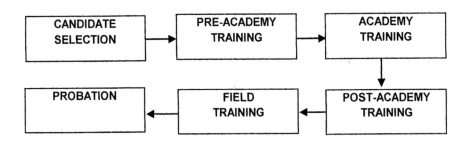

One thing the present study makes clear: stress recognition and awareness training should be mandatory for all police officers beginning at entry level. Likewise, police departments should also mandate that supervisors and executives be trained in stress recognition as well. To prevent the scenarios mentioned previously from overwhelming a police officer in the Alarm Stage, police departments should provide a realistic job preview to potential applicants. Recruits should know the exact realities of policing before they enter the academy. Without stress awareness and management training early in the candidate selection process, the department can expect individuals to be casualties of the emotional consequences of stressors that feed on themselves—growing, deepening, and ingraining over time. While many agencies offer psychological services to employees once symptoms are observed, few offer preventative training. The development of comprehensive in-service wellness and fitness programs designed to address the mental and physical health of police officers should be endorsed by police executives nationwide. Particular attention must be given to coping methods. Because time transitions may alter the perception of stress, methods to cope with its effects in a timely manner should be explored.

Inappropriate coping methods usually result during this formative period in a police officer's career and can have career-long implications if coping strategies are left solely to the discretion of the individual police officer. Many large private sector companies offer their employees stress management training. Because police work is a highly stressful occupation, police administrators must at least try to mimic private sector stress management initiatives.

Limited research has been undertaken on the subject of police officer perceived stress and police officer length of service. Further research is needed to provide information to police officers and department administrators in order for them to properly understand the dynamics of this relationship and act accordingly. Meanwhile, an internal survey can be conducted to uncover the major stressors experienced by department personnel. Police administrators may want to take advantage of this option. Police officers are generally reluctant to openly admitting that they are experiencing stress-related problems. Likewise, they are not likely to openly take issue with police administrators over intra-organizational issues that may influence their morale and performance for fear of retaliation. At the very least, the anonymous survey will allow police officers to express their feelings and provide notice to administrators about the current perceived stress levels of their individual members. It may be the chief executive officer's early warning system. The information gleaned from the survey can provide valuable insight about the situations and conditions that are problematic, and therefore stressful, to police officers. It is vitally important that identified problem areas be linked to an intervention strategy or police officers will likely view the process as a paper exercise and a farce.

Increased job satisfaction is an important ingredient in reducing stress. Although inherent job stressors cannot be changed, organizational policies and practices that tend to increase police officer perceived stress can be changed. Police administrators should consider formulating policy that will provide and maintain satisfaction with work, while at the same time reducing organizational stressors.

Along with changes in management practices, training can be tailored to better enable police officers to deal more constructively with stress. In this way the organization will be in a much better position to avoid the negative psychological and physiological consequences that stressors have on a police officer's health, morale, and productivity.

DISCUSSION QUESTIONS

1. In what stage in a police officer's career do *you* think perceived stress levels are the highest? Why?

2. In the above time stage you selected, what can be done to reduce the perceived stress occurring during this particular interval?

3. Police officers who were surveyed for a 1999 research project indicated that entry level was the period that produced the highest perceived stress levels. Why were perceived stress levels so high during this period? What can be done to alleviate this condition in the future?

4. Why would we want to conduct longitudinal studies to determine when police officers experience the highest perceived stress levels? What will be the benefits of the research to the individual, the department, and society?

Note:

The 1999 study, while useful and informative, is limited and suggests caution in generalizing the findings. The findings and conclusions, while not irrefutable, qualify them as tentative and subject to further investigation. Additional research is needed in New Jersey and other venues to ascertain if the present findings and conclusions validate the notion that a change in the previous patterns of police officer perceived stress during the transitory stages of a career has in fact occurred.

CHAPTER SEVEN
SELECTED STRESS MANAGEMENT
STRATEGIES AND COPING TECHNIQUES

OVERVIEW

Chapter Seven primarily details selected coping mechanisms and management strategies that are available to police officers suffering from the debilitating effects of perceived stress. The chapter also offers suggestions to police administrators as to how they can improve working conditions within the department, elevate police officer morale and productivity, and moderate the perceived stressors they typically experience that are related to organization itself. The narrative begins with a discussion on the subject of problem awareness, because you can't solve a problem unless you know you have one.

PROBLEM AWARENESS

People react differently to the stresses of life. Stressors provoke a wide range of reactions. Personality structures play an important role in the coping process (Kehr & Prentice, 1981). Simply stated, different things stress different people in different ways. Even so, the problems related to stress remain largely unrecognized in the beginning. They become more evident as stress levels increase.

Once the stress gets to the point where it becomes obvious, it then becomes necessary to address the predicament as quickly and as therapeutically as possible.

Because police officers are trained to deal with emergency situations, it had been assumed that they were not vulnerable to the consequences of the stress response observed in civilians. If stress symptoms occurred, it was believed that they did so only in a limited number of police officers and no special attention needed to be paid to them. In the 1980s it became clear that these assumptions were not valid (Bohl, 1995). The emotional impact of police work was understood to be complex and powerful, oftentimes beyond the individual's psychological defenses to cope with it (Bonifacio, 1991). The disturbing aspects of the job would become stressors if the individual police officer perceived them as challenging, threatening, or aversive (Mitchell & Everly, 1993).

It is acknowledged that police officers typically internalize many of the difficulties associated with stress instead of seeking professional assistance (Nowicki, 1992). Police officers historically have been reluctant to admit they are suffering from the incapacitating consequences of occupational stress. Many police officers try to deal with the stressors of their occupation by adopting a strategy that emphasizes emotional suppression (Kennedy-Ewing, 1989). Even if they are unable to cope with stress, they are not likely to reach out for help in part because they fear losing the respect of their peers or lessening their opportunities for promotional consideration (Shearer, 1993). Unfortunately, the most commonly used coping strategy is denial, a macho unwillingness to admit they are having difficulty handling stress (Mitchell & Everly, 1993; Shearer, 1993; Gentz, 1994). As a result, police officers are likely to deal with the consequences of stress inappropriately.

Over the course of their careers, police officers develop a number of behavioral traits such as cynicism, aloofness, suspiciousness, and alienation, which help them cope with the perceived stressors of the job (Evans, et al., 1992). Anderson and Bauer (1987) added that police officers often become more assertive, detached, intolerant, and manipulative as well.

Violanti and Marshall (1983) found that some police officers may respond to the pressures of the job by becoming deviant. These behaviors are likely to aggravate an already stressful condition. Shockley (1994) emphasized that police officers must successfully diffuse these antagonisms in order to avoid acting improperly and making the situation much worse. Poorly chosen coping strategies are synonymous with untreated stress. They almost always lead to stress-related illnesses, diminished quality of life, and a shorter life for police officers (Karaskek & Theorell, 1990; Reintzell, 1990).

Although the organization must have a role in stress management, individual police officers themselves are primarily responsible for taking the initiative to appropriately cope with stress. Territo & Vetter (1981) argued that the first constructive step toward coping with stress is to recognize its presence. According to Shearer (1993), a self-directed approach proven to be effective in modifying an individual's level of stress emphasizes the following practices:

- Monitoring stress levels;
- Communicating emotional pain to a significant other;
- Evaluating one's attitude toward the stressor;
- Adjusting self-expectations;
- Getting rid of psychological baggage; and
- Ensuring better physical health through diet and exercise.

A key factor in managing stress appears to be the action taken by an individual to reduce the feelings of helplessness (Howard & Joint, 1994). According to Mitchell and Everly (1993), the following cognitive techniques are also helpful in moderating perceived stressors:

- Reinterpreting failure into a success;
- Using the stressor as a valuable learning experience; and
- Considering yourself lucky that the stressor was not worse.

If competence, self-coping efficacy, and higher levels of self-esteem are associated with effectively coping with stress in the general population, it seems likely that these coping strategies will have a positive influence in dealing with the high stress associated with being a police officer (Band & Manuele, 1987).

Many law enforcement administrators fail to recognize the importance of wellness and stress management programs until an unforeseen consequence forces them to consider specific programs for reducing employee stress (Mashburn, 1993). It is fundamentally important that police administrators take a more proactive and systemic view of the causes and consequences of stress in their respective departments in order to develop effective policies and intervention strategies that can help reduce psychological distress while at the same time enhancing the morale and elevating the productivity of their police officers. Police administrators must further understand and acknowledge that a police officer's well-being is determined by a complex system of variables and relationships with no one simple solution to the problem (Hart, et al., 1995). There is no "one-size-fits-all" answer. An effective stress management program should be tailored to the individual police officer's needs. According to Bratz (1986), several constructive options are available to departments that include the following:

- Establishing a unit with the primary responsibility of counseling troubled police officers;
- Acquiring the services of a psychiatrist or psychologist;
- Periodic psychological testing; and
- Mandatory training.

The next section of the chapter identifies three intraorganizational stressors commonly associated with heightened levels of police officer perceived stress, which are represented in the following figure:

Figure 7.1: Intraorganizational Stressors.

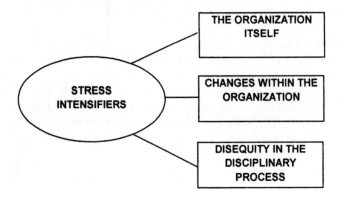

THE ORGANIZATION AS A STRESSOR

Police administrators must realize that workplace stress must be addressed as an overall organizational issue (Kottage, 1992). They must recognize their role in creating some of the perceived stressors experienced by police officers and search for ways to reduce the number of the inherent stressors that are associated with the job (Kurke, 1995). Since many of the causes and consequences of stress are directly related to the organization itself, changes within the department can do much to create a healthy workplace environment and help alleviate many of the perceived stressors experienced by police officers (Ayers & Flanagan, 1990; Alkus & Padesky, 1983). A remedy for police officer perceived stress lies in the transformation of the workplace. If such reconstruction does not take place the department may be creating an even more stressful environment that is totally incompatible with human physiological and psychological capabilities (Karasek & Theorell, 1990).

But where do we begin? Initially, the police department must consider the working conditions that inhibit and frustrate the police officer's ability to perform at optimum efficiency. According to Graves (1996), police administrators must build a culture that prevents cynicism and instead promotes a healthy, positive environment within the department; one that is principle-centered and people-oriented that encompasses a participatory management style, encourages team work, and builds self-esteem and self-worth in individuals. Karasek & Theorell (1990) wrote that organizational structures that enhance the quality of work life include democratic initiatives that allow employee involvement in decisions that directly affect them. Police officers prefer a consultative-participatory management style (i.e., involvement in policy formulation), rather than an authoritarian style (Cordner, 1978; Karasek & Theorell, 1990). Human relations are advanced when leaders share decision making with followers. Participation itself is a motivator (Jucius, 1971). People like having their opinions solicited and derive satisfaction from participating in and having some control in management decision making (Senge, 1990; Gilley, Boughton, & Maycunich, 1999).

Leaders must understand that a subordinate's commitment to a goal is in direct proportion to his or her participation in setting it. Therefore, best results occur when objectives and goals are set participatively and not simply imposed authoritatively by superiors (McCay, 1959; Hampton, Summer, & Webber, 1978; Fox, 1979; Terry & Franklin, 1982). It is self-evident that participation is also stress modifier. On the contrary, according to Gaillard and Wientjes (1994), working conditions that provide few possibilities for control and little social support are associated with increased health risks. This condition can be overcome by empowering people. It is a practice that increases one's self-confidence, self-determination, self-worth, personal effectiveness, and acts to diminish the distress associated with a perceived lack of control. Of course, a participatory management style is generally reserved for management/administrative decision making and has no place during street-level exigencies.

Figure 7.2: Situational Leadership in the Police Department.

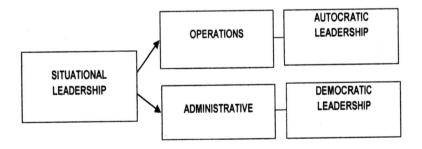

Not surprisingly, police officers who report higher job satisfaction also report significantly lower stress levels (Violanti & Aron, 1993). Police administrators play a decisive role in shaping the basic perceptions of and remedies for problems associated with police officer perceived stress (Terry, 1983). Thus, there is a need for administrators and supervisors who are sensitive to the factors that contribute to elevated stress among police officers, and who are capable and willing to develop management styles that minimize stress and enhance job satisfaction (Thrash 1990). Leadership that develops camaraderie, mutual trust and respect, and attempts to clarify organizational goals and objectives contributes to organizational commitment and work satisfaction among subordinates (Aldag & Brief, 1975; Hart, et al., 1995).

Job satisfaction contributes to overall department effectiveness. Because the department desires a reduced amount of absenteeism, fewer employee grievances, less turnover, and increased productivity, job satisfaction helps the department meet these objectives. The organization, therefore, has an incentive to lower stress and enhance job satisfaction.

Job satisfaction can be expanded in a number of ways that include the following options:

- Altering the size of the workforce to meet performance expectations;
- Rescheduling work assignments;
- Modifying policy;
- Providing job performance skill acquisition training;
- Reviewing the ergonomics of the ambient working environment; and
- Revising operational procedures that are likely to cause stress. (Luthens, 1985; Kurke, 1995).

Additional choices may include training the command staff in constructive supervisory techniques, modifying or eliminating rotating shift schedules, and improving the match between a police officer's skill, knowledge, ability, and his or her interests and personal preferences with the needs of the department (Finn & Tomz, 1997). Periodic rotation of duty assignments and other career development opportunities are mentioned as initiatives that give police officers the opportunity to learn and supplement their skills (Alkus & Padesky, 1983; Pinder, 1984; Luthens, 1985). Job rotation, for example, allows a member of the department to periodically move from one assignment to another exposing the individual to a variety of tasks that help develop skill profiles while at the same time minimizing boredom and disinterest. By rotating through the various and sundry job descriptions, the individual gains knowledge and experience and becomes familiar with many of the operations of the organization that otherwise would not come about (Voich & Wren, 1968; Deeprose, 1994; Kouzes & Posner, 1995).

CHANGE AS A STRESSOR

Although change has been a fact of life since the beginning of time, people seemingly directly or consciously resist it (Kreitner & Kinicki, 2001). Because change threatens security needs, most people tend to resist change for this very rational reason.

There seems to be an inevitable historic conflict between an individual's need for predictability and stability and the need for organizational change (Abrahamson, 2000). Change may be the most feared thing in an organization because it upsets the equilibrium. This condition worsens if the organization is in a state of constant change, because people feel powerless for the reason that they do not know what is going on (Deeprose, 1994). Change also represents inconvenience; it also disrupts working relationships and group dynamics (Kreitner & Kinicki, 2001). Each alteration requires the individual to reorient themselves. It takes time to learn new systems and to become comfortable working with new people.

Leaders are tasked with influencing followers to accept certain adjustments that are in the best interests of organizational efficiency. In order for them to be effective change agents, the organization has an obligation to prepare its leaders for their critical role in the change process. These include enumerating the responsibilities that will assist their followers in the transition *before* it occurs (Gilley, Boughton, & Maycunich, 1999). An effective leader is one who is able to encourage his or her followers to have a positive outlook while at the same time helping them overcome the anxiety associated with change. Good communication between leaders and followers will help reduce the anxiety and distress change represents. Kreitner and Kinicki (2001) suggest that leaders can become effective change agents if they consider the following suggestions:

- Change must be introduced incrementally whenever possible and with sensitivity;
- Leaders must support the change and help followers adjust by creating a state of readiness, which will help overcoming resistance to it;
- Leaders must keep followers informed about the proposed changes and the means of implementation; and
- Followers should be active participation in the change process.

BEHAVIOR CONTROL AS A STRESSOR

Motivating any workforce requires some form of behavior control. A legitimate criticism can be made that any form of behavior control is unethical if it is misapplied for selfish or devious purposes. Behavior control implies that some form of coercive power is necessary to prompt behavior that might not otherwise occur if force had not been applied (Flippo, 1971). The question becomes, "Is it ethical for one person to use coercive power to punish another person?" The use of coercive power is likely to create resentment with almost no chance of gaining follower cooperation and support if it is sought after by intimidation (Yukl, 1981). Power is all too frequently associated with exploitation, manipulation, competition, and selfishness.

The wielding of power over others is the essence of authoritarianism (Senge, 1990). Power can be said to have two faces: One side of the face is power that reflects persuasive, inspirational behavior on the part of the leader, while the other face is concerned with dominance-submission (having one's way and controlling others). One is corrective, the other is retributional. Simply stated, leaders must use the power constructively. The existence of authority does not imply the authoritarian use of it; it is an abuse of power if it involves the use of threats to bring about fear in subordinates. Power is also associated with the "I win, you lose" syndrome; that is, treating people as things to be manipulated. If power is used to dominate and subjugate subordinates, they may eventually rebel (Yukl, 1981).

DISCIPLINARY ACTION AS A STRESSOR

It is axiomatic that the possibility of disciplinary action is frightening and stressful for police officers. Even so, no rational person could suggest that disciplinary action is never needed.

Although disciplinary action may be justified, it may cause more harm than good and should be administered only when it is absolutely necessary. Even when a penalty is well-deserved, an individual will invariably accept the sanction with some amount of ill feeling. When contemplating the imposition of a punitive sanction, department leaders must recognize that such an act will invariably result in aftershocks; the negative impact will not only affect the individual (accused), but the workgroup, and the organization as well. An element of fear will likely be introduced into the psychology of the workforce if there is a perception that the disciplinary sanction imposed was administered unfairly or was used as a "weapon" by a leader against a subordinate. Who will disagree that an overemphasis on negative discipline and its associated sanctions as a form of behavior control will result in elevated stress levels in police officers, and surely will negatively influence their morale and performance?

Real or imagined unfair labor practices associated with the administration of disciplinary action can result in union grievances along with the possibility of legal action initiated by the aggrieved police officer against the department. Many of these issues arise because of the department's failure to inform its police officers what is expected of them. This is inherently unfair (Sayles &

Strauss, 1977). In sum, rules must be clearly understood and enforcement must consistent, fair, and impartial (not arbitrary and capricious) to at least have a chance of being accepted by the accused, as well as being accepted by everyone else (Hicks, 1972).

JOB BURNOUT

Another undesirable outcome of cumulative stress is burnout. Burnout can be characterized as emotional exhaustion that develops is phases. Work demands—working long hours under excessive pressure—can trigger an escape strategy that initially involves a state of psychological withdrawal from one's job (Kreitner & Kinicki, 2001). Unfortunately, burnout tends to affect the organization's hardest working and most dedicated people.

WORKPLACE HOSTILITY

Tangentially associated with cumulative stress and burnout is the potential for the manifestation of violent behavior that exists in every individual (Messier, Madden, & Mitchell, 1986). What happens to those individuals whose coping mechanism is overwhelmed by the cumulative influence of perceived stress? There is a real danger that a transfer of hostility could result in explosive and potentially violent conduct on the part of the affected individual. In the most extreme case, workplace violence can result. This reaction is characterized by either covert or overt aggression intended to damage (or in some cases destroy) the target they believe to be the cause of their frustration.

Aggression can take the form of malicious behavior (i.e., verbal abuse, gossip, initiating rumors) or rise to a level of aggression that can result in subversive conduct, vandalism to property, or physical violence directed at the target they believe to be the cause of their frustration (Pinder, 1984; Blanchard & Hersey, 1993). Aggression typically involves a normal person who experiences a temporary loss of control over their behavior. There is no exact method of predicting when a person will become violent. However, a pattern of inappropriate behavior is often an indicator of potential hostility or violence. It is a virtual certainty that one or more triggering mechanisms at the workplace can provoke consequential behavior. The answer to the question, "Can organizations kill?" is an emphatic "YES!" When a person exists in a seemingly constant state of distress, the individual is likely to reach a condition of irreconcilable frustration and the consequences to the organization could be literally disastrous.

The final segment of the chapter identifies five stress management coping techniques, which are represented in the following figure:

Figure 7.3: Stress Management Techniques.

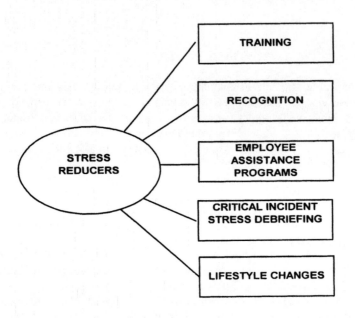

TRAINING AS A STRESS REDUCER

Stress inoculation can almost certainly be enhanced by training (Larsson & Starrin, 1988; Kureczka, 1996). Emotional survival training is essential in order to help police officers maintain their professional and private lives as normal persons and to help them avoid unnecessary emotional devastation. The most common method of preventing stress is to train police officers to recognize its sources and signs and to develop individual strategies for coping with stress (Graves 1996; Finn & Tomz, 1997). The foundation of any stress management training program must necessarily begin with a general awareness of the scope of the problem and includes the following objectives:

- To increase the police officer's understanding of the causes and consequences of stress;
- To help the police officer identify different types of stress;
- To add to the police officer's understanding of the impact of stress on his or her professional and private lives;

- To enhance the police officer's ability to prevent and cope with stress using a wide variety of strategies that include systematic relaxation, physical exercise, and behavioral structuring; and
- To provide police officers with information about the resources available to them if and when they need assistance due to stress-related consequences. (Finn & Tomz, 1997).

Ideally, stress awareness and management training should begin at entry level at the outset of a police officer's career by providing candidates with a practical and truthful job preview that details the realities of policing. Job expectations should be consistent with police work in the real world to help minimize role conflicts that will surface later on. The orientation should also include information about the routines inherent in police work as well as other aspects of the job that may be incongruent with a strict law enforcement conception that many recruits have about the job prior to entry (Teten & Mindermann, 1977; Alkus & Padesky, 1983). For sure, the actual duties of the job deviate considerably from those that are depicted on television and in the movies (Teten & Mindermann, 1977). The reality of police work actually differs somewhat from what is taught during police academy training as well (Bennett, 1984). By establishing realistic expectations early in their assimilation into the police culture, police officers are less likely to become disillusioned by the actual work (Graves, 1996). A realistic job preview has a tendency to create a higher degree of job satisfaction.

By providing accurate information, newly hired police officers will be able to determine with some precision whether or not the job will satisfy their career expectations (Teten & Mindermann, 1977).

Training police officers early in their careers to respond appropriately to perceived stressors helps prepare them for the demands of the job (Kelling & Pate, 1975). Learning how to deal with the long-term, cumulative effects of stress and how to properly cope with their consequences should begin early on as well (Reiser, 1974b). Pre-academy orientation and instruction may be the best time to begin stress management training because recruits are a captive audience and will likely retain the information throughout their entire careers (Finn & Tomz, 1977). Simulation of stressful events should take place during academy training (Kureczka, 1996). Scenario role playing helps prepare the recruit police officer for situations that will take place in the real world.

Whether before, during, or immediately after academy training, newly hired police officers should begin receiving training on the outcomes that are typically associated with responses to traumatic events. Pre-incident stress education helps to reduce the likelihood that a traumatic incident will be perceived as threatening and overwhelming (Bohl, 1995). Police officers who receive pre-incident stress training are generally better able to cope with acute stress reactions. Training promotes recovery because well-informed police officers better recognize the symptoms and are likely to seek assistance more quickly (Kureczka, 1996). In the absence of appropriate coping strategies, police officers are likely to employ schemes that include alcohol consumption or drug use, social withdrawal, and in extreme cases, acts of violence. According to Kurke (1995), proper intervention strategies increase the chances that a police officer will select coping responses that are less destructive to the individual and the department. As a result, the potential negative consequences of stressors can be minimized and police officers can become more mission-oriented and able to perform at optimum levels (More, 1992).

Mitchell and Everly (1993) made the observation that inappropriate approaches to stress reduction can create problems above and beyond stress alone. For example, since alcoholism, drug abuse, marital and family problems are viewed as by-products of perceived stress, department administrators would be wise to develop and implement a training curriculum to deal specifically with these issues and their correlates (Terry, 1983). In conjunction with the training regimen, executives and supervisors should be trained to recognize stress symptoms in their subordinates so they can act as a conduit for providing help (Kureczka, 1996).

Suicide is a worst case scenario corollary. It is a dramatic effort to communicate desperate feelings. One important indication of a potential suicide is a serious and prolonged change in a person's behavior. Danger signals include the following behavioral characteristics:

- Angry outbursts over seemingly innocuous issues;
- Loss of optimism and hope;
- Crying spells;
- Agitation;
- Poor communication; and
- A noticeable decline in performance at work. (Mitchell, 1987a).

These behavioral traits should put executives and supervisors on notice that something is seriously out-of-order; something that requires immediate intervention (Williams, 1996). Teaching executives and supervisors to recognize stress symptoms at an early stage and being familiar with the early warning signs of suicide can afford police departments the opportunity to intervene before it is too late (Lakes & Padesky, 1983; Stone, 1989; Violanti, 1995). By way of example, the Cleveland, Ohio Police Department trained lieutenants and sergeants to recognize the signs of stress in police officers.

The Cleveland Police Department's stress awareness and management program is incentive-based and rewards police officers who seek help while at the same time removing the stigma commonly associated with reaching out for support. It discourages them from keeping silent (Chapin, 2008).

Finally, family members of entry-level police officers should also receive guidance from the police department on the subject of stress awareness and management (Kureczka, 1996). Training family members not only helps the individual police officer, but it will encourage family members to become sources of support, rather than an additional cause of stress for the police officer (Finn & Tomz, 1997). Regularly scheduled workshops for police officers and their spouses can increase awareness and understanding of the stressors associated with the job and their impact on the family (Stratton, 1975). Training can prepare family members for the behavioral and life style changes that will certainly take place. The spouse should be briefed on the probable changes in attitudes and viewpoints that are typical once an individual begins a career in police work (Teten & Minderman, 1977). The information and the guidance spouses receive may help mitigate future disagreements that are likely arise between themselves and their police officer partner.

Clearly, stress awareness and management training should be an all-inclusive, department-wide initiative with an emphasis on prevention. "Prevention" should actually begin *before* an applicant is offered employment. Stress, like costs, must be contained if the organization's goals and objectives are to be achieved. Ideally, stress-prone candidates should be identified prior to their being selected for employment (Honig & Reiser, 1983). Once they are on the job the costs begin to escalate (i.e., accidents, sick leave, resignations, imposition of disciplinary sanctions, etc.). Soon after their selection for employment, stress awareness and management training should commence. On the occasion of their elevation in rank, executives and supervisors must be trained to carefully monitor the performance, conduct, and discipline of their respective subordinates.

The acquired competence will ensure that they are qualified to immediately recognize the behavioral characteristics associated with high stress levels and take the appropriate measures to make certain help is forthcoming.

RECOGNITION AS A STRESS REDUCER

Every organization is a social system. Most people have a need to be appreciated and valued as individuals. Feeling appreciated lifts employees to a higher level of job satisfaction. The most powerful non-financial motivator identified by employees is personal recognition (Kouzes & Posner, 1987). Because people do have needs other than economic, recognition becomes an important element in organizational relationships (Daniels, 1994; Nelson, 1994; Kouzes & Posner, 1995). People are energized when they receive recognition and are appreciated for their efforts (Crosby, 1979; Leboeuf, 1982; Finnigan & Schmidt, 1993; Kouzes & Posner, 1995; Gilley, et al., 1999).

Recognition needs to be integrated into the organization's formal performance appraisal process in order for individual achievement to be acknowledged. The quintessential criterion of an effective recognition scheme is that employees must know what must be done in order to earn acknowledgment and appreciation (Kreitner & Kinicki, 2001). Desired values and performance standards, therefore, must be clearly delineated (Daniels, 1994). Kouzes and Posner (1987) established three criteria for an integrated performance-reward system:

- Make certain employees know what is expected of them;
- Provide immediate positive feedback about performance; and
- Recognize and reward only those individuals who satisfy performance expectations.

Praise is an underutilized form of recognition. Because people want to have their importance clarified, praise is one of the most powerful activities a leader can perform. Catch someone doing something right and praise their effort immediately. Regardless of how it is expressed (praise, rewards, promotions, etc.), people have a need to have their importance validated (LeBoeuf, 1982; Pinder, 1984).

EMPLOYEE ASSISTANCE PROGRAMS
AS STRESS REDUCERS

Organizations can formulate plans that are capable of being designed and implemented to prevent and remediate stress (Tang & Hammontree, 1992). These applications are characteristically referred to as Employee Assistance Programs (EAPs). The purpose of the EAP is to intervene as early as possible during or immediately after the stressful situation or event, rather than trying to pick up the pieces afterward. Gershon (2009) found that appropriate interventions that address modifiable stressors and promote effective coping helps to reduce police officer stress.

EAPs often include provisions for substance abuse counseling as well as marital and family guidance and support (Shearer, 1993). They are structured to detect problems early on and help the individual resolve his or her personal difficulties (an altruistic purpose) as well as the corollaries that can influence job performance and productivity (a self-centered purpose). According to Gund and Elliot (1995), EAPs offer both the employee and the organization an opportunity to pursue the mutually beneficial goal of supporting and retaining conscientious and industrious employees. The position of the EAP should ultimately be to provide services to those who need counseling and to encourage those individuals to seek consultation and assistance when needed. According to Kurke (1995),

The goal of EAPs is three-fold: (a) resumption of adequate job performance by distressed employees; (b) improved clinical status (i.e., the recovery or rehabilitation) of distressed employees resulting from intervention; and (c) improved ability of organizational environments to function in a preventive manner, thereby reducing the occurrence of the kinds of disorders toward which the EAP interventions are directed (p. 409).

Figure 7.4: The Focuses of EAPs.

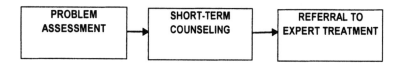

For the police department the concentration of the EAP must be the achievement of the following objectives:

- Eliminate the stressor;
- Increase the police officer's coping ability; and
- Provide the distressed police officer with help. (Kroes & Hurrel, 1975).

A pivotal reason that stressors accumulate is that many police officers do not allow themselves to express their feelings. The seemingly continuous psychological stress that some police officers experience on the job is often magnified and complicated by an inability or an unwillingness to openly discuss their personal feelings. Due to organizational and self-image factors, police officers have been historically suspicious of mental health professionals and thus are reluctant to seek their services (Alkus & Padesky, 1983). There is a tendency for police officers to be absorbed by the macho image that incorporates an emphasis on the traditional masculine role of suppressing feelings, over relying on physical prowess, and being unwilling or incapable of admitting weakness or asking for help (Curry, 1995; White & Honig, 1995).

The use of specially trained peer counselors may moderate a police officer's reluctance to reach out for help. In addition to providing instant credibility, peer counselors may offer support to police officers who might otherwise decline offers of assistance by mental health professionals. Peer counselors are usually more accessible than mental health professionals and may be better able to detect incipient stress-related problems because of their daily contact with fellow police officers (Finn & Tomz, 1997). The reluctance to talk with mental health professionals and express their emotions may be the result of the socialization practices within the police culture that shape police officer's self-perceptions. They are very likely to be concerned that fellow police officers may view them as inadequate or emotionally predisposed if they display emotion (Pogrebin & Poole, 1992). They dread the possibility of losing the respect of fellow police officers and worry about the stigma associated with seeking help.

Admitting the need for mental health support is often viewed by segments of society as a sign of weakness. Consequently, police officers are understandably fearful that sensitivity to stress and the inability to cope with stress may be interpreted by their peers and superiors as an indication of mental illness. Furthermore, police officers are concerned that admitting the need for mental health support may raise questions as to their fitness for duty (Kennedy-Ewing, 1989; Shearer, 1993; Kureczka, 1996). However, if a police officer continues to deny or repress honest emotions, the effects can escalate into a more serious psychiatric predicament (Adams, McTernan, & Remsberg, 1980). Nevertheless, many police officers experiencing mental health related issues remain reluctant to reach out for help from mental health professionals on their own (Dixon, 1988; Shearer, 1993).

Police officers may also resist professional help because they have little or no confidence in it. Moreover, they may think it demeaning to admit they need help (Clede, 1994). In view of this reluctance, the police officer's immediate supervisor may be in the best position to act as a "sounding board" in order for subordinates to express themselves, rather than suppress their emotions (Dietrich, 1989).

Supervisors thus play an important role in the front-line identification of police officers in need of counseling services. Although the police officer's job performance may be satisfactory, the immediate supervisor may be aware of subtle changes in behavior. This observation should cause the supervisor to refer the individual to an EAP when his or her behavior is out of character (Sussal & Ojakian, 1988).

A police department's proactive approach in educating police officers regarding the value of psychological assistance may significantly reduce their disinclination to reach out for help. They must be made to understand that EAPs *can* assist police officers in dealing with occupational and traumatic stressors and can effectively serve the needs of a subculture not known for accepting mental health interventions voluntarily (Gund & Elliot, 1995). By mandating psychological counseling in selected circumstances, the police department can present police officers with the opportunity to express themselves and ask questions without appearing to seek help (Kureczka, 1996). Once it is evident that a police officer is emotionally disturbed, he or she should be provided immediate access to counseling services, preferably with a full-time mental health professional or psychologist (Terry, 1983).

Once the police officer accepts the offer of psychological support services, the most important factor related to their treatment becomes the establishment of a trusting relationship between the police officer and the peer counselor, EAP agent, or the psychotherapist (Alkus & Padesky, 1983; Shearer, 1993). To achieve any level of acceptance within the police department, and in order to have a reasonable chance of success, EAPs must take sufficient care to respect the employee's right to privacy and not divulge the details of the counseling session(s) (Loo, 1986; Ostrov, Nowicki; & Beazley, 1987; Sussal & Ojakian, 1988; Kureczka, 1996). Alkus & Padesky (1983) found that issues of confidentiality arise in work with police officers. The police officer client may be particularly concerned that he or she not be seen as mentally ill or having some personal problems since the police culture firmly insists on strength and competence in all areas of the job.

Since one of the more common problems for which police officers seek treatment is marital or other relationship difficulties (Borum & Philpot, 1993), it is just as important for the police department to provide stress counseling services to family members of police officers when needed. By way of example, critical incidents can traumatize spouses and relatives almost as severely as the police officers themselves. As critical incident stress debriefing has become more common among police departments, attention is now turning to family members after an incident (Finn & Tomz, 1997). Seminars and workshops, critical incident stress debriefings for spouses and children, and psychological support services to encourage police officers and their families to seek assistance before a serious domestic problem surfaces should now be part of the department's overall goal of reducing police officer perceived stress. Because the police officer cannot help but be adversely affected by stress at home, any intervention that improves the functioning of the family will in turn improve the overall functioning of the police officer both at home and on the job (Kennedy-Ewing, 1993; White & Honig, 1995).

The death of a police officer can be traumatic for members of the department and can serve to remind other police officers of their own vulnerability. When a police officer is killed in the line of duty, the reactions of police survivors, spouses, parents, siblings, friends, and coworkers are often so profound they can be diagnosed as post-traumatic stress disorder. Survivors often endure psychological distress for long periods of time and are affected by the police department's response to the tragedy (Stillman, 1987). Unquestionably, a line-of-duty death requires the police department's immediate response to the deceased police officer's survivors. Each family has special needs and concerns when faced with such a crisis. Failure to provide continued support for the surviving family gives everyone the impression that they have been totally abandoned by the department (Sawyer, 1990). In the final analysis, by making a commitment to assist police officer families in stress management, police departments are acting in the best interest of the police officer, his or her family, the organization, and the community as a whole.

Finally, liability issues are a seemingly endless concern for contemporary police departments. According to Kureczka (1996), intervention programs can actually reduce compensation costs from potential divisive litigation. Courts have determined that police departments can be held liable for ignoring the lingering stress-related problems suffered by their police officers. Significant cash awards have been awarded to police officers whose departments failed to provide them with professional assistance when the need for support and counseling services were obvious. The interests of the department as well as the individual police officer are served by providing mental health services that are accompanied by compulsory police officer participation as necessitated by circumstance.

CRITICAL INCIDENT STRESS DEBRIEFING AS A STRESS REDUCER

Police officers frequently have to deal with acute, time-limited, stressful events. According to Mitchell and Everly (1993), critical incident or traumatic stress "represents the singlemost severe and incapacitating variation of human stress" (p. 33). The centerpiece of Post-traumatic Stress Disorder (PTSD) is the traumatic event itself, which is typically outside the usual realm of human experience that can overwhelm the victim's coping mechanisms. "PTSD represents the most incapacitating form of stress reaction" (p. 126). Because police officers are socialized to repress their emotions, they characteristically have difficulty in dealing with their feelings in the face of a traumatic event (Pogrebin & Poole, 1992). Nevertheless, it is important for police officers to seek support at the onset of symptoms, rather than let them continue (Rivers, 1993). The effects of exposure to traumatic events are like every other form of stressor in that they are cumulative (Bohl, 1995). Post-traumatic stress, however, can be mitigated by an effective Critical Incident Stress Debriefing (CISD) program within the police department.

As indicated, like so many stress management and coping strategies, rapid intervention is the key to a successful CISD. It is imperative that treatment be administered relatively soon after the traumatic event before the police officer begins to deal with the stress inappropriately. People recover better from an intensely disturbing incident if they can discharge their emotional baggage as soon as possible after the episode (Curry, 1995). Reactions have a tendency to arise within the first 24 hours. In most cases, debriefings should take place between 24 and 72 hours after the traumatic experience (Mitchell & Everly, 1993). Early cathartic intervention may provide some normalization and help minimize the expected consequences of the exposure to a traumatic event. In certain disaster situations, basic stress management techniques can be applied effectively at the scene of the incident in order to help police officers decompress. During such critical incidents peer counselors are at the scene observing emergency service responders for indications of stress overload. While on-scene defusing is particularly important in extraordinary events, a debriefing is the most often utilized strategic intervention. The basis of sound emotional help is the communication and sharing of feelings (Shearer, 1993), and this is exactly what the CISD provides.

Supervisors can effectively help reduce the duration and intensity of stress reactions subsequent to a critical incident by providing a supporting atmosphere and arranging for a CISD whenever necessary. The goal of the CISD is to mitigate the impact of the critical incident on those who were victimized by the event and to accelerate the recovery process in people who are experiencing stress after exposure to the traumatic incident (Mitchell & Everly, 1993). According to Mitchell (1986b),

> A CISD is a psychological and educational group process designed specifically for emergency workers with two purposes in mind. First, the CISD is designed to mitigate the impact of a critical incident on the personnel. Second, CISD is designed to accelerate normal recovery in normal people who are experiencing the normal signs, symptoms, and reactions to totally abnormal events (p. 25).

Mitchell (1983) characterized CISD as "an organized approach to the management of stress responses in emergency workers" (p. 37). Clark (2010) defined CISD as an organized and systematic approach to managing psychological crisis. Clark found that CISD contributes to the maintenance of good health and the productivity of police officers. CISD can be further defined as a group discussion, a verbal reconstruction of the traumatic event that provides a format for a constructive exchange of information that is structured to mitigate or resolve the psychological stress associated with the event. It allows for a ventilation of feelings. Pierson (1989) suggests that the responsible administrator mandate formal debriefings for all police officers after the incident. According to Finn and Tomz (1997), mandatory participation removes the stigma associated with counseling for the involved police officers.

CISD peer counseling is based on the Rogerian method so named for psychologist Dr. Carl R. Rogers. It is a form of encounter group in which a facilitator oversees the listening process in an attempt to create an atmosphere of warmth and acceptance. It is an arrangement which allows participants to dismiss their fears of expressing themselves. Facilitators encourage the ventilation of thoughts and feelings related to the incident. These encounter groups have great therapeutic potential. An objective of the CISD team is to foster discussion so that recovery is as rapid as possible. What is more, the CISD process allows participants to discuss the worst parts of the episode in a controlled environment that enhances the venting of emotions and prepares them for useful and appropriate stress management interventions (Mitchell, 1988).

Figure 7.5: The CISD Team.

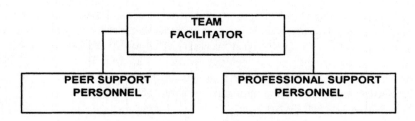

The Team Facilitator is a mental health professional who leads the CISD team; Peer Support Personnel are the emergency service workers assigned to the CISD team; and the Professional Support Personnel are mental health professionals (i.e., psychologists, psychiatric nurses, certified mental health counselors and clergy members) (Mitchell & Everly, 1993).

Stress management interventions such as CISD work for several reasons. First, if applied early they can prevent the onset of maladaptive coping mechanisms. Second, the debriefing provides the participants with an opportunity to make some sense out of what happened. Third, the debriefing has a provision for peer support. The debriefing works because it functions as a social ritual and is culturally sanctioned within the police subculture (Bohl, 1995). Solomon (1988), Kennedy-Ewing (1989), Pierson, (1989), Conroy (1990), Solomon (1990b), Mashburn (1993), Mitchell and Everly (1993), Blau (1994), and DeWolfe, Sumway, & Schmidt (1994) report that the use of peers is absolutely essential and cannot be overly emphasized because peers have a unique credibility among emergency service workers. Group support builds confidence among individuals (Terry, 1983) and peer groups provide a safe place for troubled police officers (Kureczka, 1996).

Common themes emerge during the debriefing: anger, fear of repetition of the event, powerlessness, guilt, depression, distress, questioning of career choice, and reaffirmation of efficacy and competence. The individual's feelings are validated and he or she feels less isolated (Bohl, 1995). Bohl summarized the CISD process as "Treatment [that] is brief, immediate, and directed toward the alleviation of present symptoms, prevention of future symptoms, and restoration of an earlier level of functioning" (p. 185). CISD is comprised of seven distinct phases that form the framework for the debriefing process:

Figure 7.6: The CISD Phases.

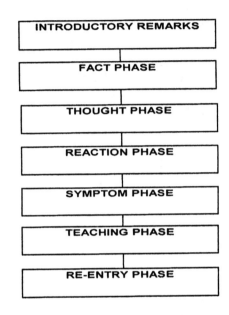

The Introductory Remarks establish the working protocol for the discussion; the Fact Phase allows the participants to describe what happened during the incident; in the Thought Phase participants are asked about their prominent thoughts during the incident; in the Reaction Phase participants discuss the elements of the incident that were the worst for them; in the Symptom Phase participants describe the indications of distress that were encountered during or after the event; in the Teaching Phase peer debriefers provide information and suggestions that can be used to reduce the impact of stress; and in the Re-entry Phase the event is summarized and the participants ask questions and offer their final thoughts (Mitchell & Everly, 1993).

To recapitulate, CISD is an attempt to stabilize a chaotic and highly stressful situation before the onset of damaging stress reactions, and to shield the victim from additional stressors by returning him or her to a pre-crisis level of functioning. The majority of reactions to critical incident stress pass within a few weeks. After 30 days, PTSD should be fading (Curry, 1995; Kureczka, 1996). However, in some cases the effects of traumatic stress may persist for several months (Rivers, 1993). The stress response is dependent on the social support the victim receives at the workplace and at home. Appropriate coping strategies for police officers are important in stress reduction and corresponding psychological adjustment (Aaron, 2000). When no adequate coping strategy is available, chronic responses may develop and linger for protracted periods of time (Galliard & Wientjes, 1994). Ultimately, the desired outcome of a CISD is a more fully functioning individual (Hanes, Stevic, & Warner, 1986; Anderson, et al., 2002).

To close the section on PTSD, it is important to incorporate a brief narrative on the consequences of a police-involved deadly force encounter. In almost every case in which a firearm is discharged in the line of duty and a death results, the police officer is relieved of his or her weapon immediately following the shooting and is treated as a homicide suspect throughout the duration of the investigation. This type of treatment often places the police officer in a condition of self-imposed isolation.

The police officer may feel betrayed by the "system." He or she may face administrative sanctions as well as criminal and civil proceedings (Cohen, 1980; Shaw, 1981). In many ways concern for the police officer's mental well-being and the psychological distress his or her family may be experiencing often receive less priority than the deadly force investigation.

When police officers are compelled to use lethal force, guilt and anxiety can be intense and overwhelming. Initially, the police officer may be dazed, inattentive, upset, and confused. He or she may experience a feeling of disbelief as well (Solomon, 1988). Nightmares, flashbacks, and severe depression are normal reactions. No matter how justified, most police officers manifest a degree of guilt or anger after a fatal confrontation (Pierson, 1988); they learn quickly that there is nothing heroic about the encounter (Cohen, 1980).

Shootings usually occur without warning and without an opportunity for the police officer to consider what, if any, alternatives are available. When a police officer seriously injures or kills another person, the stress can be so severe that much of the trauma is internalized to avoid immediate pain. This internalization of stress causes a reaction described previously as PTSD (Shaw, 1981). Victims of post-shooting trauma stress are particularly vulnerable to long term consequences of PTSD as they are likely to experience a plethora of stress reactions that include hypersensitivity, preoccupation with the event, physical symptoms, sleep deprivation, etc. that are not unlike the predictable reactions to other traumatic events (Adams, et al., 1980). According to Adams, et al. (1980), police officers tend to experience a phenomenon called "afterburn" that refers to "the tendency of the human mind to dwell on unpleasant, emotion-charged events in the wake of their actual occurrence" (p. 284). This condition is tantamount to reliving the event over and over thinking about what might have been done making the episode even more psychologically upsetting. "If you shoot and kill someone, you'll likely feel in your heart that what you did is 'bad'. . . One thing you need at this point is empathy, an understanding from other people about how you feel" (p. 288). If not mitigated appropriately, these responses could destroy a police officer's career (Cohen, 1980).

It is critical that help be given immediately after the incident. Compassion must be afforded to the involved police officer initially at the scene and judgmental remarks must be avoided thereafter (Johnson & Nowak, 1996; Finn & Tomz, 1997). Peer counseling should be made available soon afterward as it is vitally important in the recovery process (Klinger, 2006). Counseling should also be offered to the spouse and family members so they can better understand what the involved police officer will face throughout the post-shooting ordeal (Shaw, 1981).

Police officers who experience the adverse symptoms of post-traumatic combat stress must be made to realize that the symptoms will pass with time, but the length of time will vary according to the individual police officer and the nature of the incident. Unfortunately, a high proportion of police officers involved in deadly force encounters leave their respective departments because of a stress-related disability, usually within five years of the incident (Cohen, 1980). Police administrators must recognize their moral responsibility to ensure the mental well-being of the police officers under their command and institute programs to assist individuals experiencing stress related difficulties (Johnson & Nowak, 1994; Kureczka, 1996). Of course, the most effective program is one that trains police officers in what they will experience after involvement in a lethal force incident (i.e., post-shooting reactions) *before* an incident actually occurs. Once it does, the department's actions can either mitigate the stress experienced by the police officer or make it significantly worse (Klinger, 2006).

LIFESTYLE CHANGES AS STRESS REDUCERS

The most common advice given on the issue of stress management is to avoid the stimulus that causes it. Of course, in police work "avoiding the stimulus" is not possible. The more practical options include exercise, sufficient rest, a nutritious diet, attitude modification, and counseling when necessary to enhance stress defenses (Bryant, 1990; Kelly, 1997).

Exercise has long been known to promote health and reduce the influence of stressors if the physical activity is applied in a safe and reasonable manner (O'Neill, et al., 1982; Bratz, 1986; Reintzell, 1990; Mitchell & Everly, 1993). Physical conditioning prepares the body to be more resistant to the disease of stress (O'Neill, et al., 1982; Luthans, 1985). Exercise is just one of the many possible coping techniques that a police officer can employ, even though it will not eliminate stress in their lives. There are well-documented physiological benefits that accompany many forms of exercise, particularly aerobic workout routines. According to Long and Flood (1993), exercise programs facilitate the development of coping resources and are increasingly recommended as a means of protecting individuals from the deleterious effects of unavoidable work related stressors. Weekly scheduled workouts at a moderate level of intensity may yield physiological benefits, reduce acute tension and anxiety, and increase the ability to cope with perceived stress. Exercise and involvement in sports or hobbies may also serve to mitigate the negative consequences of police work and help to prevent job burnout.

Rosenbluth (1986) found that burnout can result from the severe depletion of essential chemicals due to inappropriate diet and the body's corresponding reaction to stressors. A nutritious diet enables the body to deal regularly with stressors and concomitantly limit their debilitating consequences. For example, a diet that consists of complex carbohydrates and a lessened amount of animal protein can improve the body's ability to resist a depletion of physical and emotional energy. A decrease in the consumption of salt, fatty foods, sugar, and alcohol can also add to the health benefits that are associated with a proper diet. Before beginning an exercise program or making changes to one's diet, it is always wise to consult a physician for guidance.

While exercise and diet are essential components of a healthy lifestyle, rest and relaxation are also important coping mechanisms.

Research has demonstrated that the relaxation response results in a state of lowered metabolic functioning and assists the health promoting effects of stress management (O'Neill, et al., 1982; Mitchell & Everly, 1983). Selye (1956) reported that when stress is excessive, the entire organism needs a rest; it cannot afford a struggle anywhere. Efficient work, according to Selye, is dependent in part on periodic rest and that every individual has his or her own characteristic requirements for rest and activity. Shearer (1993) wrote, "Just as a machine will show signs of wear and tear without periodic maintenance, so also does our physical system break down under chronic or prolonged stimulation" (p. 96). An exercise program combined with relaxation techniques can be invaluable as an adaptive tool in the coping process (Kehr & Prentice, 1981). According to Mitchell (1984), "Good exercise coupled with good nutrition and rest can go a long way in reducing the risk of stress-related disease" (p. 90). Consistent, routine, uniform, and predictable eating, exercise, and sleeping practices can go a long way in maintaining the health of everyone, particularly police officers who need it the most given their continuous exposure to stressors and their cumulative consequences.

As a final point, a statement on the subject of alcohol consumption must be included. Historically, alcohol consumption has been a part of the police officer's lifestyle. In moderation this practice is not necessarily unhealthy or harmful. However, in the absence of self-control, alcohol consumption is certainly not an appropriate stress management strategy or suitable coping technique (Curry, 1995). Coping with the stresses of life through alcohol use, rather than through a healthy lifestyle is counterproductive and will likely result in added sources of stress and related illnesses (Reintzell, 1990). Unfortunately, alcohol is too frequently used to relieve the effects of stress and managing its symptoms. Bonifacio (1991) reported that "Alcohol is an anesthetic to kill emotional pain"

(p. 165). The rationale behind the high rate of alcohol abuse varies from escapist drinking to peer pressure (White & Honig, 1995).

Victims of post-traumatic stress, for example, may be drawn to alcohol and drug use in order to try and diminish the intensity of the symptoms from which they are suffering. The addiction to alcohol and drugs is tantamount to a disease of emotional suppression (Adams, et al., 1980; Machell, 1993).

Administrators and executives should encourage their employees to make adjustments to their lifestyles (Kelly, 1997). Accordingly, the police department should enact positive incentives, such as higher fitness standards for retention and promotional eligibility that will serve to ensure that exercise, diet, and life style alterations become indispensable parts of a police officer's daily routine. These changes will also develop into part of the organization's comprehensive stress management plan. Support and encouragement from police associations and unions for these and similar health-related programs could do much to enhance the welfare of their members.

DISCUSSION QUESTIONS

1.   Of the various stress management strategies and coping techniques, which, in your opinion, is likely to be the most effective for police officers? Why?

2.   Are there any other reasons (not previously mentioned in this narrative) that may cause police officers to resist reaching out for assistance after experiencing a traumatic event?

3.   Why don't police officers trust mental health professionals? What can be done to overcome this preconception?

4.   Select a specific stressor and conduct a comprehensive analysis of its impact on a police officer, his or her family, the police department, and society. An appropriate coping technique must be included in the analysis.

5.   Give an example of a stressful situation to which you were exposed.

- Under what circumstance did you learn of the situation?
- What were your immediate thoughts?
- How did you react and how did you feel (physically and mentally) when confronted by the actual situation?
- What were the post-incident distressing "aftershocks" you experienced?
- What coping technique (appropriate or inappropriate) did you employ to help deal with it?

- If the same situation were to occur again, what would you do differently in terms of the response and the subsequent coping technique(s)?
- What lessons did you learn from the experience?
- What advice will you give to others if they were to be involved in a like-incident?

GLOSSARY

Burnout (also referred to as ("job burnout") is a psychological condition manifested by symptoms of suspicion, outbursts of violence, excessive consumption of alcoholic beverages, physical and emotional exhaustion, and virtual lifelessness (Kerr & Prentice, 1981). It is a general loss of feeling, concern, and a reduced level of trust, interest, and spirit (Maslach, 1982); it is an individual reaction to the effects of stress (Farber, 1983) and an exhausted psychological condition resulting from too much stress (Thrash, 1990).

Crisis is a state of emotional turmoil (Mitchell & Resnick, 1981).

Critical Incident is an event that causes a significant stressful impact upon a person sufficient enough to overwhelm an individual's usually effective coping mechanisms. Critical incidents are typically sudden, powerful events outside of the range of ordinary human experience (Mitchell & Everly, 1993) having the capacity to generate profound emotion and/or distress (Gentz, 1994). It can also be described as an abnormal event experienced by a normal individual. (Mitchell & Everly, 1993).

Critical Incident Stress is the reaction of a person to a critical incident characterized by cognitive, physical, emotional, and behavioral consequences (Mitchell & Everly, 1993).

Critical Incident Stress Debriefing is an assembly of persons who were exposed to a critical incident.
　　　A debriefing is conducted by members of a specially trained team of mental health professionals and peer support personnel that is organized and designed for the purpose of mitigating the impact of exposure to a critical incident (Mitchell & Everly, 1993).

Cynicism is an absence of idealism and an attitude of contemptuous distrust of human nature and motives (Graves, 1996).

Distress is the experiencing of specific symptoms such as anxiety and depression (Brown & Campbell, 1990).

Longitudinal Theory posits that there are transitory stages that police officers go through during their respective careers that may influence their perceptions of stress (Violanti, 1983).

Perceived Stress is the degree to which an individual interprets an experience as stressful (Brown & Campbell, 1990).

For the purpose of reference in this text, a *Police Officer* is a full-time, sworn member of an organized municipal, county, or state law enforcement agency.

Post-traumatic Stress Disorder (PTSD) is the result of a critical incident that is markedly distressing to a person and produces intense fear, terror, or helplessness (Mitchell & Everly, 1993).

Psychosomatic refers to a physical disorder caused or notably influenced by emotional factors; pertaining to or involving both the mind and the body (Webster's New Universal Dictionary, 1996).

Role Ambiguity is a condition in which a person is unclear as to what he or she is expected to do in a given situation in order to satisfy the performance expectations of the organization (Pinder, 1984).

Role Conflict is the result of competing demands or expectations that are inherently
incompatible (Pinder, 1984).

Role Stress is a perceived imbalance between social demands and perceived response capability under conditions where failure to meet demands has important consequences (Violanti, 1983); anything about an organizational role that produces adverse consequences for an individual (Kahn & Quinn, 1970).

Strain is the result of the negative mental, behavioral, and physical outcomes of stress (Stotland, Pendleton, & Schwartz, 1989).

Stress is a non-specific response of the body to any demand; the more significant the demand, the more intense the reaction (Selye, 1956). It is the perceived imbalance between societal demands and response capabilities (Violanti, 1983; Sigler & Wilson, 1988). It is a condition in which some variable or combination of variables on the job interacts with the worker to disrupt his or her psychological equilibrium (Kroes & Hurrel, 1975). It is a self-perceived negative or unpleasant impact upon an individual (Brown & Campbell, 1990).

Stressors are the antecedents of stress that act as a stimulus placing a demand upon a person (Mitchell & Everly, 1993).

REFERENCES

Aaron, J.D.K. (2000). Stress and coping in police officers. *Police Quarterly,* Vol. 3, No. 4: 438-450.

Abrahamson, Eric. (2000). Changes without pain. *Harvard Business Review,* (July-August, 2000).

Adams, R.J., McKernan, T.M., & Remsberg, C. (1980). *Street Survival: Tactics For Armed Encounters.* Northbrook, IL: Calibre Press.

Albrecht, S. (1992). Beating burnout: Don't let the streets get you down. *Texas Police Journal,* 40(11): 1-3.

Aldag, R.J., & Brief, A.P. (1975). Supervisory style and police role stress. *Journal of Police Science and Administration,* 6(3): 362-368.

Alkus, S., & Padesky, C. (1983). Special problems of police officers: Stress related issues and interventions. *The Counseling Psychologist,* 11(2): 55-64.

Anderson, G.S., Litzenberger, R., and Plecas, D. (2002). Physical evidence of police officer stress. *Policing: An International Journal of Police Strategies & Management,* Vol. 25, Issue 2: 399-420.

Anderson, W., & Bauer (1987). Law enforcement officers: The consequences of exposure to violence. *Journal of Counseling and Development,* 65(7): 381-384.

Anderson, W., Swenson, D., & Clay, D. (1995). The psychology of stress. *Stress Management for Law Enforcement,* 37-38.

Arcuri, A.F. (1976). Police pride and self-esteem: Indications of future occupational changes. *Journal of Police Science and Administration,* 4(4): 436-444.

Arcuri, A.F. (1977). You can't take fingerprints off water: Police officers' view of "cop" television shows. *Human Relations,* 3(1): 237-247.

Axelberd, M., & Valle, J. (1978). Stress control program for police officers. City of Miami Police Department. Unpublished concept paper #1, Counseling and Stress Control Center.

Ayers, R.M., & Flanagan, G.S. (1990). *Preventing Law Enforcement Stress: The Organization's Role.* Washington, D.C.: U.S. Government Printing Office. In Boyd, J.S. (1994). *Police officer stress and police officer length of service.* PhD dissertation, College Station, TX: Texas A&M University.

Babin, M. (1980). Perceiving self-destructive responses to stress: Suicide and alcoholism. *RCMP Gazette,* 42(7-8): 20-22.

Bahn, C. (1984). Police socialization in the eighties: Strains in the forging of an occupational identity. *Journal of Police Science and Administration,* 12(6): 390-394.

Ball, S. (1986). Self-defeating behavior patterns in law enforcement officers. *Psychological Services for Law Enforcement.* Washington, D.C.: U.S. Government Printing Office.

Band, S.R., & Manuele, C.A. (1987). Stress and police officer performance: An examination of effective coping behavior. *Police Studies,* 10(3): 122-131.

Barath, I. (2009). Stress management research at the Ontario Police College. *The Police Chief,* Vol. 76, Issue 8 (August 2009): 112-114, 116-121.

Barocas, B., Canton, A.N., Li X., and Vlahov, D. (2009). Mental, physical, and behavioral outcomes associated with perceived work stress in police officers. *Criminal Justice and Behavior,* Vol. 36, No. 3: 275-289.

Bartol, C.R., Bergen, G.T., Volckens, J.S., & Knoras, K.M. (1992). Women in small-town policing: Job performance and stress. *Criminal Justice and Behavior,* 19(3): 240-259.

Bedeian, A.G., & Armenakis, A.A. (1981). A path-analytic study of the consequences of role conflict and ambiguity. *Academy of Management Journal,* 24(2): 417-424.

Bennett, R.R. (1984). Becoming blue: A longitudinal study of police recruit occupational socialization. *Journal of Police Science and Administration,* 12(1): 47-58.

Beuter, L., Nussbaum, P., & Meredith, K. (1988). Changing personality patterns of police officers. *Professional Psychology Research and Practice,* 19(5): 503-507. In Boyd, J.S. (1994). *Police officer stress and police officer length of service.* PhD dissertation. College Station, TX: Texas A&M University.

Blackmore, J. (1978). Are police allowed to have problems of their own? *Police Magazine,* 1(3): 47-55.

Blanchard, Kenneth H., & Hersey, P. (1993). *Management Of Organizational Behavior: Utilization Of Human Resources.* (6th Ed.). Prentice-Hall, Inc., Englewood Cliffs, New Jersey.

Blau, T.H. (1994). *Psychological Services for Law Enforcement.* New York: John Wiley & Sons.

Bohl, N. (1992). Hostage negotiator stress. *FBI Law Enforcement Bulletin,* 61(8): 23-26.

Bohl, N. (1995). Professionally administered critical incident stress debriefing for police officers. In Kurke, M.I., & Scrivner, E.M. (Eds.). *Police Psychology Into the 21st Century,* (pp. 169-188). Hillsdale, N.J.: Lawrence Erlbaum Associates.

Boles, J.S., Johnston, M.W., & Hair, J.F., Jr. (1997). Role stress, work-family conflict and emotional exhaustion: Inter-relationships and effects on some work-related consequences. *Journal of Selling and Sales Management,* 17(1): 17-28.

Bonifacio, P. (1991). *The Psychological Effects of Police Work: A Psychodynamic Approach.* New York: Plenum Press.

Borum, R., & Philpot, C. (1993). Therapy with law enforcement couples: Clinical management of the high risk life style. *American Journal of Family Therapy,* 21(2): 122-135.

Boyd, J.S. (1994). *Police officer stress and length of service,* PhD dissertation, College Station, TX: Texas A&M University.

Bratton, W., with Knobler, P. (1998). *Turnaround: How America's Top Cop Reversed the Crime Epidemic.* New York: Random House.

Bratz, L. (1986). Combating police stress. *FBI Law Enforcement Bulletin,* (January): 2-7.

Brooks, L.W., Piquero, A., & Cronin, J. (1994). Work-load rates and police officer attitudes: An examination of busy and slow precincts. *Journal of Criminal Justice,* 22(3): 277-286.

Brown, J.M., & Campbell, E.A. (1990). Sources of occupational stress in the police. *Work and Stress,* 4: 305-318.

Brown, J.M., & Campbell, E.A. (1994). *Stress and Policing: Sources and Strategies.* Chichester: John Wiley & Sons.

Brown, J., Cooper, C., & Kirkcaldy, B. (1996). Occupational stress among senior police officers. *British Journal of Psychology,* 87(1): 31-41.

Brown, M.K. (1981). *Working The Street: Police Discretion and the Dilemmas of Reform*. New York: Russell Sage Foundation.

Bryant, C. (1990). Law enforcement stress: I need help. *National FOP Journal*, 19(2): 10-11, 57-58.

Bureau of National Affairs. (1986). *Alcohol and Drugs in the Workplace: Costs, Controls, and Controversies*. A BNA Special Report, Washington, D.C.

Burke, R.J. (1989). Career stages, satisfaction, and well-being among police officers. *Psychology Reports*, 65: 3-12.

Chapin, M., Brannen, S.J., Singer, M.I., & Walker, M. (2008). Training police leadership to recognize and address occupational stress. *Police Quarterly*, 11(3): 338-352.

Clark, D.W., and Healey, M. (2010). Crisis response tools for law enforcement. *The Police Chief*, (February, 2010).

Clede, B. (1994). Stress, insidious or traumatic, is treatable. *Law and Order*, (January, 1994).

Cohen, A. (1980). I've killed a man ten thousand times. *Police Magazine*, (July): 17-22.

Collins, P.A., & Gibbs, A.C.C. (2003). Stress in police officers: A study of the origins, prevalence, and severity of stress-related symptoms within a county police force. *Occupational Medicine*, Vol. 53: 256-264.

Conroy, D.L., & Hess, K.M. (1992). *Officers At Risk: How To Identify and Cope With Stress*. Costa Mesa, CA.: Custom Publishing Company.

Conroy, R.J. (1990). Critical incident stress debriefing. *FBI Law Enforcement Bulletin*, 59(2): 20-22.

Cordner, G.W. (1978). The review of work motivation theory and research for the police manager. *Journal of Police Science and Administration*, 6(3): 286-292.

Crank, J.P., & Caldero, M. (1991). Production of occupational stress in medium-sized police agencies: A survey of line officers in eight municipal departments. *Journal of Criminal Justice*, 19(4): 339-349.

Crank, J.P., Regoli, B., Hewitt, J.D., & Culbertson, R.G. (1993). An assessment of work stress among police executives. *Journal of Criminal Justice*, 21: 313-324.

Crosby, A. (1979). The psychological examination in police selection. *Journal of Police Science and Administration*, 7(2): 215-229.

Crosby, P.B. (1979). *Quality Is Free: The Art of Making Quality Certain*. McGraw-Hill Book Company, New York.

Curry, L. (1995). Reducing trauma after the event. *People Management*, 9: 38-41.

Daniels, A.C. (1994). *Bringing Out The Best In People: How To Apply The Astonishing Power of Positive Reinforcement*. New York: McGraw-Hill, Inc.

Daniello, R.J. (1999). Police officer perceived stress and police officer length of service. DPA dissertation. Fort Lauderdale, Florida: Nova-Southeastern University.

Danto, B.L. (1978). Police suicide. *Police Stress*, 1(1): 32-36, 40.

Dantzer, M.L. (1987). Police-related stress: A critique for future research. *Journal of Police and Criminal Psychology*, 3(3): 43-48.

Darien, Andrew (2002). The alter ego of the patrolman? Policewomen and the discourse of difference in the NYPD. *Women's Studies*, Vol. 31, Issue 5 (September/October 2002): 561-608.

Dash, J., & Reiser, M. (1978). Suicide among police in urban law enforcement agencies. *Journal of Police Science and Administration*, 6(1): 18-21.

Davidson, M.J., & Veno, A. (1980). Stress and the policeman. In Cooper, C.L., & Marshall, J. (Eds.). *White Collar and Professional Stress,* (pp. 131-166). Chichester: John Wiley & Sons.

Deeprose, Donna (1994). *How To Recognize & Reward Employees.* AMACOM: American Management Association, the WorkSmart series, New York.

Deeter-Schmelz, D.R., & Ramsey, R.P. (1997). Considering sources and types of social support: A psychometric evaluation of the House and Wells (1978) instrument. *Journal of Personal Selling and Sales Management,* 17(1): 49-61.

Delattre, E.J. (1989). *Character and Cops: Ethics in Policing.* Washington, D.C.: American Enterprise Institute for Public Policy Research.

Dement, W.C. (1976). *Some Must Watch While Some Must Sleep: Exploring The World of Sleep.* W.W. Norton & Company, New York, London.

Denyer, T., Callender, T., & Thompson, D. (1975). The policeman as alienated laborer. *Journal of Police Science and Administration,* 3(3): 251-258.

DeWolfe, D.J., Sumway, G., & Schmidt, G. (1994). Metro Transit's trauma response. *Employee Assistance,* 7(3): 27-33.

Dietrich, J.F., & Smith, J. (1986). The non-medical use of drugs including alcohol among police personnel: A critical literature review. *Journal of Police Science and Administration,* 14(4): 300-306.

Dietrich, J.F. (1989). Helping subordinates face stress. *The Police Chief,* (November): 44-47.

DiVasto, P., & Saxton, G. (1992). Munchausen's syndrome in law enforcement. *FBI Law Enforcement Bulletin,* (April): 11-14.

Dixon, K. (1988). Employee assistance programs: A primer for buyer and seller. *Hospital and Community Psychiatry,* 39(6): 623-627.

Dyas, R.D. (1959). The mental miasma—A police personnel problem. *Police,* (July/August): 65-69.

Eisenberg, T. (1975). *Job stress and the police officer: Identifying stress reduction techniques, job stress, and the police officer.* Proceedings of Symposium, Cincinnati, Ohio, (May 8-9): 26-34. Washington, D.C.: U.S. Government Printing Office.

Ellison, K.W., & Genz, J.L. (1983). *Stress and the Police Officer.* Springfield, IL.: Charles C. Thomas.

Evans, B.J., Coman, G.J., & Stanley, R.O. (1992). The police personality: Type A behavior and trait anxiety. *Journal of Criminal Justice,* 20: 429-441.

Farber, B.A. (1993). (Ed.). *Stress and Burnout in Human Service Professions.* New York: Paragon Press.

Farmer, R.E. (1990). Clinical and managerial implications of stress research on the police. *Journal of Police Science and Administration,* 17(3): 205-218.

Fell, R.D., Richard, W.C., & Wallace, W.L. (1980). Psychological job stress and the police officer. *Journal of Police Science and Administration,* 8: 139-143.

Finn, P., & Tomz, J.E. (1997). *Developing a Law Enforcement Stress Program for Officers and Their Families.* Washington, D.C.: U.S. Department of Justice, Office of Justice Programs, National Institute of Justice.

Finnegan, J.P., & Schmidt, W.H. (1993). *TQM Manager: A Practical Guide For Managing In A Total Quality Organization.* Jossey-Bass Publishers, San Francisco.

Fletcher, C. (1990). *What Cops Know.* New York: Pocket Books.

Flippo, E.B. (1971). *Principles Of Personnel Management.* (3rd Ed.). McGraw-Hill Book Company, New York.

Fox, D. (1979). *Managing The Public's Interest: A Results-oriented Approach.* Holt, Rinehart, and Winston, New York.

Freudenberger, H.J. (1974). Staff burnout. *Journal of Social Issues,* 30: 159-165.

Freedy, J.R., & Hobfoll, S.E. (1994). Stress inoculation for reduction of burnout: A conservation of resources approach. *Anxiety, Stress, and Coping,* 6: 311-325.

Gallard, A.W.K., & Wientjes, C.J.E. (1994). Mental load and work stress as two types of energy mobilization. *Work and Stress,* 8(2): 141-152.

Garner, G.W. (1994). When the shooting is over: Emotional survival in a deadly force scenario. *Police and Security News,* 10(6): 3, 5-7.

Gentz, D. (1994). Critical incident reactions: A comparison of two studies ten years apart in the same police department. *Journal of Police and Criminal Psychology,* 10(2): 35-37.

Gershon, R.M., Barocas, B., Canton, A.N., Li, X., & Vlahov, D. (2009). Mental, physical, and behavioral outcomes associated with perceived work stress in police officers. *Criminal Justice and Behavior,* 36(3), (June): 229-231.

Gibbs, N. (1994). Officers on the edge. *Time,* 144(13), (September 26): 62-64.

Gilley, J.W., Boughton, N.W., & Maycunich, A. (1999). *The Performance Challenge: Developing Management Systems To Make Employees Your Organization's Greatest Asset.* Perseus Books, Reading, Massachusetts.

Goodin, C.V. (1978). Opening remarks. In Kroes, W.H., & Hurrell, J.J. (Eds.). *Job Stress and the Police Officer: Identifying Stress Reduction Techniques,* (pp. 1-2). Washington, D.C..: U.S. Government Printing Office.

Graf, F.A. (1986). The relationship between social support and occupational stress among police officers. *Journal of Police Science and Administration,* 14(5): 178-186.

Graham-Bonnalie, F.E. (1972). *The Doctor's Guide To Living With Stress.* New York: Drake Publishers, Inc.

Grant, M.G. (1977). The relationship of moonlighting to job dissatisfaction in police officers. *Journal of Police Science and Administration,* 1977: 193-196.

Graves, W. (1996). Police cynicism: Causes and cures. *FBI Law Enforcement Bulletin,* (June): 16-20.

Green, R.E., & Reed, B.J. (1988). Occupational stress and mobility among professional local government managers: A decade of change. *The Municipal Yearbook 1988,* published by the International City Management Association.

Grennan, S.A. (1987). Findings on the role of gender in violent encounters with citizens. *Journal of Police Science and Administration,* 15(1): 78-85.

Griggs, D.F. (1985). Police stress and management style. *Dissertation Abstracts International,* 46(4A): 1094.

Gudjonsson, G.H., & Adlam, R. (1985). Occupational stressors among British police officers. *Police Journal,* 58: 73-85.

Gund, N., & Elliott, B. (1995). Employee assistance programs in police organizations. In Kurke, M.I., & Scrivner, E.M. (Eds.). *Police Psychology into the 21st Century,* (pp. 149-167). Hillsdale, N.J.: Lawrence Erlbaum Associates.

Hageman, M.J.C. (1978). Occupational stress and marital relationships. *Journal of Police Science and Administration,* 6(4): 402-412.

Haisch, D.C., & Meyers, L.S. (2004). MMPI-2 assessed post-traumatic stress disorder related to job stress, coping, and personality in police agencies. *Stress and Health,* Vol. 20, No. 4 (October 2004): 223-229.

Hall, H.J. (1969). Police work is a family affair. *Law & Order*, (September): 43-44, 46, 48.

Hammett, T. (1987). *AIDS and the Law Enforcement Officer: Concerns and Policy Responses, Issues, and Practices*. Washington, D.C.: U.S. Department of Justice, National Institute of Justice.

Hampton, D.R., Summer, C.E., & Webber, R.A. (1978). *Organizational Behavior and the Practice of Management*. (3rd Ed.). Scott, Foresman, and Company, Glenview, Illinois.

Hansen, J.C., Stevic, R.R., & Warner, R.W. Jr. (1972). *Counseling Theory and Process*, Boston: Allyn and Bacon, Inc.

Hardy, M.E., & Conway, M.E. (1978). *Role Theory: Perspectives for Heatlh Professionals*. New York: Appleton-Century-Crofts.

Harpold, J.A., & Feemster, J.D. (2002). Negative influences of police stress. *FBI Law Enforcement Bulletin*, Vol. 71, Issue 9. (Sept. 2002): 1-7.

Hart, P., Wearing, A.J., & Headey, B. (1993). Assessing police work experiences: Development of the police daily hassles and uplift scales. *Journal of Criminal Justice*, 21(6): 553-572.

Hart, P., Wearing, A.J., & Headey, B. (1995). Police stress and well-being: Integrating personality, coping and daily work experiences. *Journal of Occupational and Organizational Psychology*, 68(2): 133-157.

He, N., Zhao, J., & Ren, L. (2005). Do race and gender matter in police stress?: A preliminary assessment of the interactive effects. *Journal of Criminal Justice*, Vol. 33, Issue 6. (November/December, 2005): 535-547.

Heinman, M.F. (1975). The police suicide. *Journal of Police Science and Administration*, 3(3): 267-273.

Hicks, H.G. (1972). *The Management of Organizations: A Systems and Human Resources Approach*. (2nd Ed.). McGraw-Hill Book Company, New York.

Hillgren, J.S., Bond, R., & Jones, S. (1976). Primary stressors in police administration and law enforcement. *Journal of Police Science and Administration,*. 4(4): 45-49.

Honig, A., & Reiser, M. (1983). Stress disability pension experience in the Los Angeles Police Department; A historical study. *Journal of Police Science & Administration*, 11(4): 385-388.

House, R.J, & Rizzo, J.R. (1972). Toward the measurement of organizational practices: Scale development and validation. *Journal of Applied Psychology*, 56: 388-396.

Howard, A., & Joint, M. (1994). Fatigue and stress in driving. *Employee Counseling Today*, 6(6): 3-7.

Howard, W.G., Donofrio, H.H., & Boles, J.S. (2004). Inter-domain work-family, family work conflict, and police work satisfaction. *Policing: An International Journal of Police Strategies & Management*, Vol. 27, Issue 3: 380-395.

Hurrel, J.J. (1986). Some organizational stressors in police work and means for their amelioration. In Reese, J.T., & Goldstein, H.A. (Eds.). (1986). *Psychological Services for Law Enforcement*, (pp. 449-452). Washington, D.C.: U.S. Government Printing Office.

Jackson, S., & Maslach, C. (2007). After-effects of job-related stress: Families of victims. *Journal of Organizational Behavior*, Vol. 3., Issue 1. (Sept. 2007): 63-77.

Jacobi, J.H. (1975). Reducing police stress: A psychiatrist's point of view. In Kroes, W.H., & Hurrell, J.J. (Eds.). *Job Stress and the Police Officer: Identifying Stress*

Reduction Techniques, (pp. 85-116). Washington, D.C.: U.S. Government Printing Office.

Janik, J. (1990). Fear of fear itself. In *Fear: It Kills! A Collection of Papers for Law Enforcement Survival.* Produced by the International Association of Chiefs of Police. Arlington, VA.

Jaramillo, F., Nixon, R., & Sams, D. (2005). The effect of law enforcement stress on organizational commitment. *Police: An International Journal of Police Strategies & Management,* Vol. 28, Issue 2: 321-336.

Johnson, B.R., & Nowak, P. (1996). Stress and officer-involved shootings: The agency's responsibility. *The Police Chief,* (September): 42-44.

Johnson, L.B. (1991). Job strain among police officers: Gender comparisons. *Police Studies,* 14(1): 12-16.

Jucius, M.J. (1971). *Personnel Management.* (7th Ed.). Richard D. Irwin, Inc., Illinois.

Kahn, R.L., Wolfe, D.M., Quinn, R.P., Snoek, J.D., & Rosenthal, R.A. (1964). *Occupational Stress: Studies in Role Conflict and Ambiguity.* New York: John Wiley & Sons, Inc.

Kahn, R.L., & Quinn, R.P. (1970). Role stress: A framework for analysis. In Crank, J.P., Regoli, B., Hewitt, J.D., & Culbertson, R.G. (1993). An assessment of work stress among police executives. *Journal of Criminal Justice,* 21: 313-324.

Kannady, G. (1993). Developing stress-resistance police families. *The Police Chief,* 4(8): 92-95.

Karasek, R., & Theorell, T. (1990). *Healthy Work Stress, Productivity, and the Reconstruction of Working Life.* New York: Basic Books, Inc.

Kaslof, L.J. (1992). Police stress: The hidden assailant. *Advances,* 6(1): 20-22.

Kaufmann, G.M., & Beehr, T.A. (1989). Occupational stressors, individual strains, and social support among police officers. *Human Relations,* 42(2): 185-197.

Kay, S. (1994). Why women don't apply to be police officers. *The Police Chief,* (April): 44-45.

Kedjidjian, C. (1995). How to combat workplace stress. *Safety & Health,* 151(4): 36-41.

Kehr, B., & Prentice, M. (1981). Cop burnout – A stressful situation. *Nautilus Magazine,* (April/May): 36-37.

Kelling, G., & Pate, M. (1975). The person-role fit in policing: Current knowledge and future research. In Kroes, W.H., & Hurrell, J.J. (Eds.). *Job Stress and the Police Officer: Identifying Stress Reduction Techniques.* (pp. 117-129). Washington, D.C.: U.S. Government Printing Office.

Kelly, J.M. (1997). Get a grip on stress. *Human Resource Management,* 42(2): 51-55.

Kennedy-Ewing, L. (1989). *Occupational and Training Guide for the Critical Incident Stress Management Program of Delaware County, PA.* Department of Human Resources, Media, PA.

Klein, R. (1989). Police peer counseling. *FBI Law Enforcement Bulletin,* (October): 1-4.

Klinger, D. (2006). *Police Response to Officer-involved Shootings.* National Institute of Justice, the Research, Development, and Evaluation Agency of the U.S. Department of Justice. (January 2006). No. 253.

Kohan, A., & Mazmanian, D. (2003). Police work, burnout, and pro-organizational behavior. *Criminal Justice and Behavior,* Vol. 30, No. 5: 559-583.

Kottage, B.E. (1992). Stress in the workplace. *Professional Safety,* (August, 1992): 24-26.

Kouzes, J.M., & Posner, B.Z. (1995). *The Leadership Challenge: How To Keep Getting Extraordinary Things Done In Organizations.* Jossey-Bass, A Wiley Company, San Francisco.

Kreitner, R., & Kinicki, A. (2001). *Organizational Behavior.* (5th Ed.). Irwin McGraw-Hill, Boston.

Kroes, W.H., Margolis, B.L., & Hurrell, J.J.,Jr., (1974a). Job stress in policemen. *Journal of Police Science and Administration,* 2(2): 145-155.

Kroes, W.H., Margolis, B.L., & Hurrell, J.J.,Jr., (1974a). Job stress in police administrators. *Journal of Police Science and Administration,* 2(4): 381-388.

Kroes, W.H. (1974). *Psychological Stress and Police Work.* Unpublished presentation at the Third Annual Stress Symposium of the American Academy of Stress, 1974.

Kroes, W.H., & Hurrell, J.J. (1975). Stress awareness. In Kroes, W.H., & Hurrell, J.J. (Eds.). *Job Stress and the Police Officer: Identifying Stress Reduction Techniques.* (pp. 234-245). Washington, D.C.: U.S. Government Printing Office.

Kroes, W.H. (1976). *Society's Victim: The Policeman.* Springfield, IL: Charles C. Thomas.

Kroes, W.H. (1985). *Society's Victim – The Policeman: An Analysis of Job Stress In Policing.* (2nd Ed.). Springfield, IL: Charles C. Thomas.

Kureczka, A.W. (1996). Critical incident stress in law enforcement. *FBI Law Enforcement Bulletin,* 65(2-3): 10-17.

Kurke, M.I. (1995). Organizational management of stress and human reliability. In Kurke, M.I., & Scrivner, E.M. (Eds.). *Police Psychology Into the 21st Century.* (pp. 391-415). Hillsdale, N.J.: Lawrence Erlbaum Associates.

Langner, T.J. (1962). A twenty-two item screening test of psychiatric symptoms indicating impairment. *Journal of Health and Human Behavior,* 3: 269-276.

Larsson, G., & Starrin, B. (1988). Appraisal and coping processes in acute time-limited stressful situations: A study of police officers. *European Journal of Personality,* 2: 259-276.

Lazarus, R., Folkman, S., & DeLonis, A. (1988). The impact of daily stress on health and mood: Psychological and social resources as mediators. *Journal of Personality and Social Psychology,* 54(3): 486-495.

LeBoeuf, M. (1982). *The Productivity Challenge: How To Make It Work For America And You.* McGraw-Hill Book Company, New York.

Lefkowitz, J. (1977). Industrial-organizational psychology and the police. *American Psychologist,* 32(5): 346-364.

Lester, D. (1983). Why do people become police officers? *Journal of Police Science and Administration,* 11(2): 170-174.

Long, B.C., & Flood, K.R. (1993). Coping with work stress: Psychological benefits of exercise. *Work and Stress,* 7(2): 109-119.

Loo, R. (1986). Police psychology: The emergence of a new field. *The Police Chief,* (February): 26-30.

Luthans, F. (1985). *Organizational Behavior.* (4th Ed.). New York: McGraw-Hill Book Company.

Machell, D.F. (1993). Combat post-traumatic stress disorder, alcoholism, and the police officer. *Journal of Alcohol and Drug Education,* 38(2): 23-32.

Mantell, M.R. (1986). San Ysidro: When the badge turns blue. In Reese, J.T., & Goldstein, H.A. (Eds.). *Psychological Services for Law Enforcement,* (pp. 357-360). Washington, D.C.: U.S. Government Printing Office.

Manuel, L.L., Retzlaff, P., & Sheehan, E. (1993). Policewomen personality. *Journal of Social Behavior and Personality*, 8(1): 149-153.

Martelli, T.A., Waters, L.K., & Martelli, J. (1989). The police stress survey: Reliability and relation to job satisfaction and organizational commitment. *Psychological Reports*, 64: 267-273.

Martin, C.A., McKean, H.E., & Veltkamp, L.J. (1986). Post-traumatic stress disorder in police and working with victims: A pilot study. *Journal of Police Science and Administration*, 14(2): 98-101.

Martin, D. (1994). Cops and counseling. *Law Enforcement Technology*, 21(5): 50-51.

Martin, M., Marchand, A., Boyer, R., & Martin, N. (2009). Predictors of the development of post-traumatic stress disorder among police officers. *Journal of Trauma & Dissociation*, Vol. 10, Issue 4 (Oct-Dec 2009): 451-468.

Martin, S. (1980). *Breaking And Entering: Policewomen On Patrol.* Berkeley: University of California Press.

Mashburn, M.D. (1993). Critical incident counseling. *FBI Law Enforcement Bulletin*, 62(9): 5-8.

Maslach, C. (1982). *Burnout – The Cost of Caring.* New Jersey, Prentice-Hall.

Mattison, S. (1990). The fear factor in law enforcement. In *Fear: It Kills! A Collection of Papers for Law Enforcement Survival.* Produced by the International Association of Chiefs of Police. Arlington, VA.

Maynard, P.E., & Maynard, N.W. (1980). Preventing family stress through couples communication training. *The Police Chief*, 47: 30-31.

McCafferty, F.L., Domingo, G.D., & McCafferty, M.J. (1989). Understanding post-traumatic stress disorder. *The Police Chief*, (February): 22-24.

McCarthy, R. (1990). The dynamics of police-related fears: Reasonable and unreasonable fear. In *Fear: It Kills! A Collection of Papers for Law Enforcement Survival.* Produced by the International Association of Chiefs of Police. Arlington, VA.

McCay, J.T. (1959). *The Management of Time.* Prentice-Hall, Inc., Englewood Cliffs, N.J.

McFarlane, A.C., & Bryant, R.A. (2007). Post-traumatic stress disorder in occupational settings: Anticipating and managing the risk. *Occupational Medicine*, 57(6): 404-410.

Meagher, M.S., & Yentes, N.A. (1986). Choosing a career in policing: A comparison of male and female perceptions. *Journal of Police Science and Administration*, 14(4): 320-327.

Messier, L.D., Madden, D.J., & Mitchell, J.T. *Violence in Field Situations.* In Mitchell, J.T., & Resnick, H.L.P. (1996). *Emergency Response to Crisis: A Crisis Intervention Guidebook for Emergency Service Personnel.* Jeffrey T. Mitchell, Ph.D., Ellicott City, Maryland.

Minirth, F., & Meier, P. (1992). *The Stress Factor.* Chicago, IL.: Northfield Publishing Company.

Mitchell, J.T., & Resnik, H.L.P. (1981). *Emergency Response to Crisis.* Maryland: Jeffrey T. Mitchell, PhD.

Mitchell, J.T. (1983). When disaster strikes . . . The critical incident stress debriefing process. *JEMS*, (January): 36-39.

Mitchell, J.T. (1984). High tension: Keeping stress under control. *Firehouse*, (September): 86-88, 90.

Mitchell, J.T. (1986a). Assessing and managing the psychologic impact of terrorism, civil disorder, disasters, and mass casualties. *ECQ,* 2(1): 51-58.

Mitchell, J.T. (1986b). Critical incident stress management. *Response!,* (September/October): 24-25.

Mitchell, J.T. (1987a). By their own hand. *Chief Fire Executive,* (January/February): 48, 50-52, 65, 72.

Mitchell, J.T. (1987b). Effective stress control at major incidents. *Maryland Fire and Rescue Bulletin,* (June): 3, 6.

Mitchell, J.T. (1988). Development and functions of a critical incident stress debriefing team. *JEMS,* (December): 43-46.

Mitchell, J.T., & Everly, G.S. Jr. (1993). *Critical Incident Stress Debriefing (CISD): An Operations Manual for the Prevention of Traumatic Stress Among Emergency Services and Disaster Workers.* Ellicott City, Maryland: Chevron Publishing Corporation.

Morash, M., & Haarr, R.N. (1995). Gender, workplace problems, and stress in policing. *Justice Quarterly,* 12: 113-140.

Morash, M., Haarr, R., & Kwak, D. (2006). Multi-level influences on police stress. *Journal of Contemporary Criminal Justice,* Vol. 22, No 1: 26-43.

More, H.W. (1992). Reaction to police work: Stress and its consequences. In *Special Topics In Policing.* (pp. 171-218). Cincinnati, OH.: Anderson Publishing Company.

Mosher, D. (1988). Overcoming employee's fears about EAPs. *EAP Digest,* (July/August): 102-103.

Moyer, I.L. (1986). An exploratory study of role distance as a police response to stress. *Journal of Criminal Justice,* 14: 363-373.

Muir, W.K. (1977). *Police: Streetcorner Politicians.* Chicago: University of Chicago Press.

Mullen, J. (1998). Job advice to cut police absenteeism. *People Management,* 4: 15-16.

Nelson, B. (1994). *1001 Ways To Reward Employees.* Workman Publishing, New York.

Niederhoffer, A. (1967). *Behind The Shield: The Police In Urban Society.* New York: Anchor, Doubleday & Co.

Norvell, N., Belles, D., & Hills, H. (1988). Perceived stress levels and physical symptoms in supervisory law enforcement personnel. *Journal of Police Science and Administration,* 16(2): 75-79.

Nowicki, E. (1992). *True Blue: True Stories About Real Cops.* Power Lake, WI.: Performance Dimensions Publishing.

Nye, R.D. (1986). *Three Psychologies: Perspectives From Freud, Skinner, and Rogers.* (3rd Ed.). Monterey, CA.: Brooks/Cole Publishing Company.

O'Neill, J.L., & Cushing, M.A. (1991). *Impact of Shift Work on Police Officers.* Washington, D.C.: Police Executive Research Forum.

O'Neill, M.W., Hanewicz, W.B., Fransway, L.M., & Cassidy-Riske, C. (1982). Stress inoculation training and job performance. *Journal of Police Science and Administration,* 10(4): 388-397.

Ostrov, E. (1986). Police/law enforcement psychology. *Behavioral Sciences & the Law.* 4(4): 353-370.

Palahunic, L., McCafferty, F., & Domingo, G. (1989). Manifestations of PTSD in police officers. *Police Chief,* 56(2): 24-28.

Parker, L.C., & Roth, M.C. (1973). The relationship between self-disclosure personality and a dimension of job performance of policemen. *Journal of Police Science and Administration,* 1(3): 282-287.

Paterson, B.L. (1992). Job experience and perceived job stress among police, correctional, and probation officers. *Criminal Justice and Behavior,* 19(3): 260-285.

Paul, G.N. (1990). The climate of fear in law enforcement. In *Fear: It Kills! A Collection of Papers for Law Enforcement Survival.* Produced by the International Association of Chiefs of Police. Arlington, VA.

Pendleton, M., Stotland, E., Spiers, P., & Kirsch, E. (1989). Stress and strain among police, firefighters, and government workers. *Criminal Justice and Behavior,* 16(2): 196-210.

Pierson, T. (1988). Critical incident stress and the tactical team. *The Tactical Edge,* (Summer): 26-27.

Pierson, T. (1989). Law enforcement stress: A serious law enforcement problem. *The Police Chief,* (February): 32-33.

Pinder, C.C. (1984). *Work Motivation: Theory, Issues, and Applications.* Glenview, IL.: Scott, Foresman, & Co.

Pogrebin, M.R., & Poole, E.D. (1992). Police and tragic events: The management of emotions. *Journal of Criminal Justice,* 19: 395-403.

Pogrebin, M.R., & Poole, E.D. (1993). Vice isn't nice: A look at the effects of working undercover. *Journal of Criminal Justice,* 21(4): 383-394.

Prunckun, H.W. (1991). Police culture and stress. *Criminology in Australia,* 2(4): 10-13.

Rack, D.M., Lawley, T., & Ingram, R. (1976). Are police recruits cynical? *Journal of Police Science and Administration,* 4(3): 352-359.

Reese, J. (1986). Policing the violent society: The American experience. *Stress Medicine,* 2: 233-240.

Reese, J., Horn, J., & Dunning, E. (Eds.). (1991). *Critical Incidents In Policing.* Washington, D.C.: U.S. Government Printing Office.

Reintzell, J.F. (1990). *Police Officer's Guide To Survival, Health, and Fitness.* Springfield, IL.: Charles C. Thomas.

Reiser, M. (1974a). Some organizational stress on policemen. *Journal of Police Science and Administration,* 2(2): 156-159.

Reiser, M. (1974b). Mental health in police work and training. *Police Chief,* 4(10): 51-52.

Reiser, M. (1975). Stress, distress, and adaptation in police work. In Kroes, W.H., & Hurrell, J.J. (Eds.). *Job Stress and the Police Officer: Identifying Stress Reduction Techniques.* (pp. 17-25). Washington, D.C.: U.S. Government Printing Office.

Resier, M. (1978). The problem of police officers' wives. *The Police Chief,* 45: 38-42.

Reiser, M., & Geiger, S. (1984). The police officer as a victim. *Professional Psychology: Research and Practice,* 15(3): 315-323.

Richard, W.C., & Fell, R.D. (1975). Health factors in police job stress. In Kroes, W.H., & Hurrell, J.J. (Eds.). *Job Stress and the Police Officer: Identifying Stress Reduction Techniques.* (pp. 73-84). Washington, D.C.: U.S. Government Printing Office.

Rivers, K. (1993). Traumatic stress: An occupational hazard. *Employee Counseling Today,* 5(1): 4-6.

Robbins, S.P., & Judge, T.A. (2007). *Organizational Behavior.* (12th Ed.). Pearson Prentice Hall. Upper Saddle River, New Jersey.

Robinette, H.M. (1987). *Burnout In Blue: Managing The Police Marginal Performer.* New York: Praeger.

Rommetveit, R. (1954). *Social Norms and Roles.* Minneapolis: University of Minnesota Press.

Rosenbluth, E.S. (1986). Police burnout—increasing durability to stress illness through the body's own chemistry. In Reese, J.T., & Goldstein, H.A. (Eds.). *Psychological Services for Law Enforcement.* (pp. 501-513). Washington, D.C.: U.S. Government Printing Office.

Saatoff, G.B., & Buckman, J. (1990). Diagnostic results of psychiatric evaluations of state police officers. *Hospital and Community Psychiatry,* 41(4): 429-432.

Sawyer, S. (1990). *Support Services to Surviving Families of Line-of-Duty Death: A Public Safety Agency Handbook.* Concerns of Police Survivors, Inc.

Sayles, L.R., & Strauss, G. (1977). *Managing Human Resources.* Prentice-Hall, Inc. Englewood Cliffs, N.J.

Scanlon, R.A. (1990). Police enemy #1: Stress. *Law Enforcement Technology,* 17(4): 18-21.

Schaefer, R. (1985). Maintaining control, a step toward personal growth. *FBI Law Enforcement Bulletin,* 10: 14. In Boyd, J.S. (1994). *Police officer stress and police officer length of service.* PhD dissertation. College Station, TX: Texas A&M University.

Selye, H. (1956). *The Stress of Life.* (Rev. Ed.). New York: McGraw-Hill Book Company.

Senge, P.M. (1990). *The Fifth Discipline: The Art and Practice of the Learning Organization.* Currency Doubleday, New York.

Sewell, J. (1981). Police stress. *FBI Law Enforcement Bulletin,* (April): 7-11.

Shaw, J.H. (1981). Post-shooting trauma: Effective measures to deal with the delayed stress reaction. *The Police Chief,* (June): 58-59.

Shaw, J.B., & Barrett-Power, E. (1997). A conceptual framework for assessing organization, work group, and individual effectiveness during and after downsizing. *Human Relations,* 50(2): 109-127.

Shearer, R.W. (1993). Police officer stress: New approaches for handling tension. *The Police Chief,* 60(4): 96-99.

Shockley, S.M. (1994). Fit for duty; Mad as hell. *Police,* 18(9): 20-21, 90.

Sigler, R.T., & Wilson, C.N. (1988). Stress in the workplace: Comparing police stress with teacher stress. *Journal of Police Science and Administration,* 16(3): 151-162.

Singleton, G.W., & Teahan, J. (1978). Effects of job related stress on the physical and psychological adjustment of police officers. *Journal of Police Science and Administration,* 6: 355-361. In Pita, M.E. (1993). *Stress and burnout in police officers.* PhD dissertation. Washington, D.C.: The George Washington University.

Sklansky, D.A. (2006). Not your father's police department: Making sense of the new demographics of law enforcement. *The Journal of Criminal Law & Criminology,* Vol. 96, Issue 3, (Spring 2006): 1209-1243.

Solomon, R.M. (1988). Post-shooting trauma. *The Police Chief,* (October): 40, 42, 44.

Solomon, R.M. (1990a). The dynamics of fear in critical incidents: Training implications. In *Fear: It Kills! A Collection of Papers for Law Enforcement Survival.* Produced by the International Association of Chiefs of Police. Arlington, VA.

Solomon, R.M. (1990b). Administrative guidelines for dealing with officers involved in on-duty shooting situations. *The Police Chief,* (February): 40.

Southworth, R.N. (1990). Taking the job home. *FBI Law Enforcement Bulletin,* (November): 19-23.

Spielberger, C.D., Wetbury, L.G., Geier, K.S., & Greenfield, G. (1981). *The Police Stress Survey: Sources of Stress in Law Enforcement.* Human Resource Institute Monograph Series. 3(6). Tampa, FL.: University of South Florida, College of Social and Behavioral Sciences.

Standfest, S.R. (1996). The police supervisor and stress. *FBI Law Enforcement Bulletin,* May: 7-10.

Stearns. G.M., & Moore, R.J. (1993). Physical and psychological correlates of job burnout in the Royal Canadian Mounted Police. *Canadian Journal of Criminology,* (April): 127-148.

Steers, R.M. (1981). *Introduction To Organization Behavior.* Glenview, IL.: Scott, Foresman.

Stillman, F.A. (1987). Line-of-duty deaths: Survivor and departmental responses. *National Institute of Justice, Research in Brief,* (January): 1-5.

Stinchcomb, J.B. (2004). Searching for stress in all the wrong places: Organizational stressors in policing. *Police Practice and Research,* Vol. 5, Issue 3, (July 2004): 259-277.

Stone, R.W. (1989). Stress in the police service. *Police Journal,* 61(2): 151-154.

Storch, J.E., & Panzarella, R. (1996). Police stress: State-trait anxiety in relation to occupational and personal stressors. *Journal of criminal Justice,* 24(2): 99-107.

Stotland, E., Pendleton, M., & Schwartz, R. (1989). Police stress, time on the job, and strain. *Journal of Criminal Justice,* 17: 55-60.

Stotland, E. (1991). Effects of police work and professional relationships on health. *Journal of Criminal Justice,* 19(4): 371-380.

Stratton, J.G. (1975). Pressures in law enforcement marriages. *Police Chief,* 42: 44-47.

Stratton, J.G. (1978). Police stress: an overview. *Police Chief,* 45(4): 58-62. In Boyd, J.S. (1994). *Police officer stress and police officer length of service.* PhD dissertation. College Station, TX.: Texas A&M University.

Stratton, J.G. (1984). *Police Passages.* Manhattan Beach, CA.: Glennon Publishing Company.

Sussal, C.M., & Ojakian, E. (1988). Crisis intervention in the workplace. *Employee Assistance Quarterly,* 4(1): 71-85.

Symonds, M. (1969). *Emotional hazards of police work.* Paper presented to the American Psychiatric Association on May 8, 1969.

Tang, T., & Hammontree, M. (1992). The effects of hardiness, police stress, and life stress on police officers' illness and absenteeism. *Personnel Management,* 21: 493-515.

Territo, L., & Vetter, H.J. (1981). Stress and police personnel. *Journal of Police Science and Administration,* 9(2): 195-208.

Terry, G.R., & Franklin, S.G. (1982). *Principles of Management.* (8th Ed.). Richard D. Irwin, Inc., Homewood, Illinois.

Terry, W.C. III (1981). Police stress: The empirical evidence. *Journal of Police Science and Administration,* 9(1): 61-95.

Terry, W.C. III (1983). Police stress as an individual and administrative problem: Some conceptual and theoretical difficulties. *Journal of Police Science and Administration,* 11(2): 156-165.

Teten, H.D., & Minderman, J.W. (1977). Police personnel problems—Practical considerations for administrators. *FBI Law Enforcement Bulletin,* (January): 8-15.

Thompson, B.M., Kirk, A., & Brown, D.F. (2005). Work based support, emotional exhaustion, and spillover of work stress to the family environment: A study of policewomen. *Stress and Health*, Vol. 21, Issue 3. (August): 199-207.

Thrash, P.D. (1990). How to deal with BOSS: Burnout stress syndrome. *Law Enforcement Technology*, 17(5): 26-28, 30.

Van Maanen, J. (1973). Observations on the making of policemen. *Human Organizations*, 32: 407-418.

Van Maanen, J. (1975). Police socialization: A longitudinal examination of job attitudes in an urban police department. *Administration Science Quarterly*, 20(2): 207-228.

Van Maanen, J. (1995). Kinsmen in repose: Occupational perspectives of patrolmen. In *Police and Society: Touchtone Readings*, (1995). (pp. 225-242). Prospect Heights, IL.: Waveland Press.

Vila, B. (2009). *Sleep Deprivation: What Does it Mean for Public Safety Officers?* National Institute of Justice. U.S. Department of Justice Programs, Office of Justice Programs. No. 262.

Violanti, J. (1983). Stress patterns in police work: A longitudinal study. *Journal of Police Science and Administration*, 11: 211-216.

Violanti, J., & Marshall, J. (1983). The police stress process. *Journal of Police Science and Administration*, 2: 389-394.

Violanti, J.M., Vena, J.E., & Marshall, J.R. (1986). Disease risk and mortality among police officers: New evidence and contributing factors. *Journal of Police Science and Administration*, 14(1): 17-23.

Violanti, J.M. (1988). Operationalizing police stress management. In Reese, J.T., & Horn, J.M. (Eds.). *Police Psychology: Operational Assistance*. (pp. 423-435). Washington, D.C.: Federal Bureau of Investigation.

Violanti, J.M., & Aron, F. (1993). Sources of police stressors: Job attitudes, and psychological distress. *Psychological Reports*, 72: 899-904.

Violanti, J.M., & Aron, F. (1994). Ranking police stressors. *Psychological Reports*, 75: 824-826.

Violanti, J.M. (1995). Mystery within: Understanding police suicide. *FBI Law Enforcement Bulletin*, 64(2): 19-23.

Violanti, J., & Aron, F. (1995). Police stressors: Variations in perception among police personnel. *Journal of Criminal Justice*, 23(3): 287-294.

Violanti, J.M. (2004). Predictors of police suicide ideation. *Suicide and Life-threatening Behavior*, Vol. 34, Issue 3. (Fall 2004): 277-283.

Voich, D., & Wren, D.A. (1968). *Principles of Management: Resources and Systems*. The Ronald Press Company, New York.

Vulcano, B., Barnes, G., & Breen, L. (1984). The prevalence of psychosomatic disorders among a sample of police officers. *Social Psychiatry, 19(4): 181-186*

Washington, Crime News Service (1975). Compensation for police heart attacks allowed. *Crime Control Digest*, 9(10): 3.

Webb, S.D., & Smith, D.L. (1980). Police stress: A conceptual overview. *Journal of Criminal Justice*, 8: 251-257.

Weiser-Remington, P. (2005). Women in the police: Integration or separation? *Qualitative Sociology*, Vol. 6, Issue 3. (August 2005): 199-207.

Weiss, D., & Fagan, J. (2002). Police officers who experience traumatic event have greatest risk of PTSD. University of California. 02(11).

Westmoreland, B., & Haddock, B.D. (1989). Code 3 driving: Psychological and physiological stress effects. *Law and Order,* 37(11): 29-31.

Wexler, J.G., & Logan, D.D. (1983). Sources of stress among women police officers.
Journal of Police Science and Administration, 11(1): 46-53.

White, E.K., & Honig, A.L. (1995). Law enforcement families. In Kurke, M.I., & Scrivner, E.M. (Eds.). *Police Psychology Into the 21st Century.* (pp. 189-206). Hillsdale,
N.J.: Lawrence Erlbaum Associates.

Williams, H. (1996). Cops on the edge. *Nieman Reports,* 50(3): 38-39.

Williams, C. (2003). Sources of workplace stress. *Perspectives on Labor and Income, the
Online Edition,* Vol. 4, No 6. (June 2003).

Wilson, O.W., McLaren, R.C., Fyfe, J.J., Greene, J.R., & Walsh, W.F. (1997). *Police
Administration.* (5th Ed.). New York: McGraw-Hill Companies, Inc.

Witkin, G., Geist, T., & Friedman, D. (1990). Cops under fire. *US News and World Report,* 109(22): 32-44.

Wittrup, R.G. (1986). Police shooting—an opportunity for growth or loss of self. In
Reese, J.T., & Goldstein, H.A. (Eds.). *Psychological Services for Law Enforcement,*
(pp. 405-408). Washington, D.C.: U.S. Government Printing Office.

Yerkes, R., & Didson, J. (1908). The relation of strength of stimulus to rapidity of habit
formation. *Journal of Comparative and Neurological Psychology,* 18: 459-482.

Yukl, G.A. (1981). *Leadership In Organizations.* Englewood Cliffs, N.J.: Prentice-Hall,
Inc.

INDEX

Absence from the home *17*
Absenteeism *ix, xvi, xvii, 64*
Accountability *32*
Action Imperative Syndrome *52*
Administrative support *26-29, 31*
Aggression *67*
Alarm Stage *50*
Alcohol and drug dependency *9, 45, 70, 82-83*
Alienation *4, 13, 27, 29, 60*
Antidote to job stress *18*
Attitude of distrust *15*
Autocratic organizational structure *26*
Authoritarianism *15, 54, 66*

"Bad" stress *xvi, 8*
Behavioral and performance expectations *28, 34, 54, 64, 72*
Behavioral traits *60, 70*
Behavior control *66-67*
Budget constraints *26, 31*
Burnout *25, 67, 82*

Candidate selection process *54-55*
Career development *29, 64*
Catastrophes *41*
Causes and consequences of stress *xvi, 61-62, 68*
Change *65*
Chronic stress *2*
Circadian rhythms *36, 54*
Cleveland (OH) Police Department stress management program *70*
Coercive power *66*
Combat trauma *43*
Communications *26*

Computer in-car use *47*
Computerized information management *46-47*
Conception of justice *11, 21*
Conflicting expectations *20*
Constitutional constraints *20*
Constructive fear *38-39*
Coping with fear *39*
Court decisions *21*
Courts *21-22*
Criminal justice system *11, 21*
Crisis *43*
Critical incident *20*
Critical incident stress *40-43*
Critical incident stress debriefing *75-76*
Critical incident stress debriefing phases *79*
Critical incident stress debriefing team *78*
"Culture shock" *54*
Cumulative stress *44-45*

Deadly force encounter *43, 80-81*
Death of coworker *41, 75*
Decision making process *7*
Denial *41, 60*
Department policy *7, 28, 44*
Depersonalization *40, 53*
Deviance *60*
Diet *xv, 60, 81-83*
Disciplinary practices *16, 26, 31, 66-67*
Discussions with family *12-13*
Disenchantment Stage *50-51*
Distress *9, 16, 25, 38, 41-43, 61*
Downsizing *27*

Dysfunction and disease *xvi, 3, 46*

Educational attainment *32*
Emergent situations *17*
Emergency driving *37*
Emergency responses *40*
Emerging issues *46-47*
Emotional impact *xvii, 59*
Emotional suppression *17, 53, 60, 83*
Employee assistance programs *72-76*
Employee relations *27*
Employer responsibilities *55*
Environmental hazards *7*
Errors *xvii*
Ethnic minority members *29-30*
Executive stress *31-32*
Exercise *xv, 60, 69, 81-83*
Excessive paperwork *26*
Exhibited behavior within the family *11-18*
Exposure to fear and danger *12*
Extreme weather conditions *7*

Family member counseling *75*
Fatigue *4, 7, 37, 38*
Fault-finding *27*
Fear *38-39*
Female member role expectations *29*
Fight-or-flight response *4, 37-38*
Financial status *16*
"Fishbowl Effect" *20*
Fitness for duty *74*
Functional failures *3*

Gender and minority stress *29-30*
General Adaptation Syndrome *3*
Goal of stress management *9*
"Good" stress *1-2*
Group cohesiveness *28*
Group stressors *22*

Growth and development *29, 64*

Health maintenance *81-82*
Hostage and barricaded persons *41, 44*

Impact of stress *xvi*
Inadequate pay *26*
Inadequate resources *26, 31*
Inappropriate coping mechanisms *9, 55, 60, 78*
Individual (unique) reactions to stress *45*
Individual stressors *33-47*
Inherent stressors *5-9, 58*
Internal conflict *19*
Intervention *61, 70, 72, 74-78*
Intragroup stressors *11-23*
Intrinsic dangers *6*
Introspection Stage *51*
Investigation of misconduct *16*
Irregular and unpredictable hours *17, 26, 36-37*

Job burnout *25, 67, 82*
Job itself *23*
Job participation *27-28, 63, 65*
Job-related stress *xv, xvi, 7*
Job satisfaction *xv, xvi, 28, 56, 64*

Labor practices *66*
Leader as change agent *65*
Length of service (perceived stress) *49-56*
Lethal force *44, 80-81*
Liability issues *76*
Lifestyle changes *81-83*
Line-of-duty death *16, 75*
Longitudinal Theory *49-51*
Loss of victim *34, 41*

Management information technology *46-47*

Mandating psychological counseling *74*
Marital discord *11, 18*
Marital distancing *18*
Media reports *20*
Mental Health Professionals *73-74, 78*
Misplaced emotions *17*
Mitigation strategies *49, 68-71, 83*
Morale *xvi, 27, 29, 61*
Motivation *2, 32*
Multi-casualty incident *41*

Nature of the job *8*
Neglect *xvii*
Nutrition *82*

Occupational demands of the job *20*
Occupational environment *7*
Occupational risks *14*
Occupational stressors *5, 16, 20*
Operation of a motor vehicle *7*
Organization *25, 61-62*
Organizational and interpersonal stressors *25-32*
Overprotective *15*

Paramilitary structure *15, 26*
Patrol operations *7, 33, 37-39*
Peer counselors *73, 77*
Peer group *9, 14, 78*
Perceived public disapproval of police *21*
Perceived stress in the Alarm Stage *50*
Perception of stress *2*
Performance *xvi*
Performance evaluations *26, 31, 72*
Performance expectations *28-29, 40*
Personalization Stage *50*
Persuasive power *66*

Pessimism *15, 36*
Phases of a crisis *43*
Physical and psychological consequences *1-4*
Physical conditioning *81*
Police culture *69, 74-75*
Police image *15, 20, 53, 73*
Police officer (def) *86*
Police work as high stress occupation *5*
Political support *26*
Poor supervision and poor leadership *26*
Post-shooting trauma stress *80-81*
Post-traumatic combat stress *43-44*
Post-traumatic Stress Disorder *46, 75-76*
Praise *72*
Pre-academy orientation *69*
Privacy *75*
Problem awareness *59-61*
Professional standards *28*
Promotional practices *26, 29*
Psychological support services *75*
Psychosomatic *1, 2*
Public expectations *20, 42*
Public support *21, 26, 52*
Punitive sanctions *17, 66*

Rapid intervention *76*
Reaction to traumatic events *17*
Realistic job preview *55, 69*
Realities of police work *xv, 5-9*
Reasons for wanting to be a police officer *5-6*
Recidivism *21*
Relationship with children *16*
Relationship with family and friends *11-18*
Relationship with management *27-28*
Reluctance to seek help *73-74*

Relying exclusively on other police
officers *13-14*
Removal of gun after deadly force
incident *43*
Repetitive job stressors *46*
Rest and relaxation *82*
Rewards, recognition, and promo-
tions *29*
Right to privacy *75*
Rogerian Method *77*
Role ambiguity *6, 19-20*
Role as family member *13*
Role conflict *18-21*
Role of a police officer *19*
Role playing (scenarios) *69*
Rotating shifts *36-37, 64*

Safety *xvii*
Salary and benefits *16*
Scandals *16*
Self-imposed isolation *21*
"Sequential Traumatization" *45*
Situational leadership *63*
Sleep deprivation *xv, 9, 33, 36-37*
Social service agency *22*
Social structures *18*
Social support *14, 32, 41, 63*
Socialized behavior *13-15*
Sources of role stress *11, 19*
Special duty assignment *17*
Special operations *44*
Stages of a police officer's career
49-56
State of constant readiness *8, 65*
Stigma *39, 70, 74, 77*
Strain *8, 14, 37, 53*
Stress awareness *55, 69-71*
Stress (def) *xvi*
Stress management and coping
techniques *59-83*
Stress management program *61*
Stress-provoking assignments *6-7*
Stressors (def) *87*

Stress survey *55-56*
Subculture *14, 21, 74*
Substance abuse counseling *72*
Suicide *18, 41, 70*
Suicide gesture *45*
Supervisor's role in stress man-
agement *70, 74, 77*
Supervisor stress *32*
Supervisor-subordinate relation-
ships *22, 28-29, 32, 47*
Supervisor support *28*
Suppression of feelings *60*
Suspicion *15*
Suspiciousness *15, 60*
Synopsis of 1999 longitudinal
study *51-52*

Threat of injury or death *16*
Training family members *71, 72,
75*
Training programs *49, 68-71*
Transformation of the workplace
62
Trauma stress *40, 43-46, 80*
Type "A" behavior *23, 33-34*
Type "A" personality *33-34*

Union grievances *66*
Unrealistic job expectations *52*
"Us-versus-them" view of society
13
Unwarranted fear *38*

"Vulnerability Awareness" *38, 42*

Wearing the uniform *52*
Wellness programs *55*
Women in policing *29-30*
Work-family conflicts *11*
Work responsibilities and family
obligations *11-18*
Work schedule *xv, 17, 26, 33, 36-
37*

Workforce reductions *27*
Working conditions *7, 11, 26-27,
62-63*
Working the street *5, 28, 31, 34,
37-38, 50*

Workload *33, 36*
Workplace hostility *67*
Workplace violence *67*

ABOUT THE AUTHOR

Robert J. Daniello is a former police officer who served for over 30 years with the Cherry Hill, New Jersey Police Department from 1968 to 1998 retiring with the rank of Captain and the title of Division Commander. Upon retirement, Robert J. Daniello worked for two years as a consultant to local government with the State of New Jersey Treasury Department. He is currently a consultant and adjunct faculty member at the School of Administrative Science, Farleigh Dickinson Univeristy, Hackensack, New Jersey.

Robert J. Daniello has earned five college degrees including a Doctorate in Public Administration, and is a Certified Public Manager in New Jersey. He served seven years as a member of the Critical Incident Stress Debriefing Team Network of New Jersey during the 1990s.